WATCHING MOVIES, WATCHING STORIES:

AN INTERACTIVE GUIDE FOR ENGAGING CULTURE THROUGH FILM

TROY KINNEY

PHOENIX, ARIZONA

Scripture quotations are from The ESV® Bible (The Holy Bible, English Standard Version®, copyright© 2001 by Crossway, a publishing ministry of Good News Publishers. Used by permission. All rights reserved.

Troy Kinney
Phoenix, Arizona/85027
www.troykinney.com
tk@troykinney.com

Book Layout ©2017 BookDesignTemplates.com

Watching Movies, Watching Stories/ Troy Kinney. —1st ed.
Dynamic QR codes added March, 2021 –2nd ed.
ISBN-13:978-1723370700
ISBN-10:1723370703

Contents

i

Dedicated to my wife

ACKNOWLEDGMENTS

I would like to give my thanks to the many people that offered encouragement and advice alongside my journey of writing this first book. I especially want to thank my friend Randy Kutz for challenging me in the first place to write down what I was already teaching. I want to thank my mom and my wife for being the first to dive into the text and fix all my spelling errors and grammar issues. Thanks also needs to go to my lifelong friend Richard J. Klaus for accepting the challenge of commenting through an early copy of the text. I also want to thank Eric Saar for his valuable input. Thank you to Walter and Megan Lindsay for your love and no-nonsense comments. Thanks to my mother-in-law Janet Gray for also going through my later manuscript and cleaning off the stray threads. I also want to thank the folks at the 2017 Southern California Christian Writers Conference for your encouragement as I explained my ideas in starting this project. The reassurance I received really helped me gain momentum. Lastly, I want to thank Valerie Coulman, whom I met at the conference, for understanding my vision and being my editor.

The televisor is 'real.' It is immediate, it has dimension. It tells you what to think and blasts it in. It must be, right. It seems so right. It rushes you on so quickly to its own conclusions your mind hasn't time to protest...

–Ray Bradbury, *Fahrenheit 451*

[1]

APOLOGIA

MANY OF US CHRISTIANS go through life acting like the mission field is somewhere out there or over there. We compartmentalize our lives and feel ill-equipped to unwrap a conversation about spiritual or religious issues with our co-workers over our sandwich and pre-packaged salad.

This guide is designed to equip you to both analyze the movies and media most of us watch and to use that as a springboard to not only deepen your understanding, but to create engaging discussions with those we spend time with. I want to utilize the things we watch to open avenues for you to talk about spiritual truths. Many of us binge on seasons of this and episodes of that on a regular basis. The proliferation of media streaming services like Netflix, Amazon Prime Video, Hulu, Sling, Crackle and the ubiquity of screens and internet make it a good bet that the people we work with, sit next to in cafés, and live next to are all watching the same movies and shows that we are watching. These are all people we should be talking with, and many of us need more to talk about than just the weather and sports. We should be offering truth in love and hope.

I want to equip you with some tools to watch film. These tools will be presented throughout this guide, first for us to understand the movies we are watching, and then for us to engage with the people in our lives; for us to participate in truly meaningful conversations, dealing with ideas that affect us as human beings and as believers. I ultimately offer this guide in the hopes that we can turn our interactions with all towards the Bible and Jesus.

This guide is intended to familiarize you with many of the common techniques, jargon, and other means used in the visual media's trade. I do this with the help of video clips throughout the text. Once you get a grasp of those ideas you can begin to use them to create conversation about the messages inherent in all visually creative works.

The guide is designed to be completed alone, in a small group, or with your family. The subject matter and material discussed is for adults and mature teens. Through questioning strategies and discussion topics, I want to create a kind of dialogue and stimulate discussion, reflection and learning. I intend to do this through providing a variety of film clips, some of my own ideas, and ideas I have picked up along the way. To offer you a real reel experience, high-speed internet access will be necessary. I have created an interactive text which will allow you to have a real-time visual of the movie clips that illustrate the ideas and terminology I am presenting. It includes both <u>clickable hyper-links</u> for e-readers and **QR codes** for smart phones throughout the book. QR codes are the unique square symbols throughout. With newer smart phones, you simply use your camera and place the QR code in the visible area on your screen A link should appear on your phone that you touch or click. Sometimes for your phone to read these symbols it will require a QR Reader App on your smart mobile-device (there are many free ones available). Both will allow you to view the film clips I use for discussion. *At the time of this writing, all links were working through the companies and channels that are hosting them.*

The most important key to the understanding of a film is an understanding of your own standards. For the writing of this guide I have made one key assumption and that is that Jesus Christ and the Bible have authority over your life. If you do not have a standard like the Bible to measure other world views against, it will be difficult for you to discern between the benefits or pitfalls of other philosophies.

It has been said that there are no right or wrong answers, as if anything is possible. I believe this statement is flawed. I say: **There are wrong answers, but there may be various plausible good answers and great ideas**. For this reason, you will encounter many open-ended questions in the chapters ahead. These types of questions may frustrate some but they are designed for discussion and reflection.

This guide is designed for people who are Christ-believers and are currently watching the films and/or television shows that are shown in the world. It is not a treatise or defense of any particular film. I try not to make judgements about whether a movie is okay or is not okay for any person or group of people to watch. I understand that individuals may have issues with bad language, violence, skin (nudity and sex) and political/social agendas and I am not demanding anyone watch movies he or she feels will cause stumbling. **There are no clips with sex or nudity**. I may reference movies with ratings of G, PG, PG-13, and R but I have attempted to keep all clips and discussions as "clean" as possible. Having said that, the film clips included here may have scenes of violence or "PG-13" type language that some may find offensive or inappropriate.

I am not anyone's conscience, just like a rating system isn't either. I am not going to apologize for films made by human hands, but I am also not giving license to say that all or any of the movies referenced are entirely okay to watch by anyone at any time. I only suggest that as believers, discernment should be employed in the watching of all films.

[2]

OVERTURE

BEING IN THE WORLD BUT NOT OF IT

IT WAS MAY OF 1977. The weather in Phoenix was starting to really warm up and so was the summer movie season. I remember waiting outside the Harkin's Cine Capri with my parents and younger brother. I was seven and I sat on the sidewalk next to the brass stanchions slung with red velvet ropes that loosely hugged the line of folks waiting for the next show. My parents thought it would be funny to tell me we were seeing *The Shaggy DA* starring Dean Jones. My brother had seen that the week before and I had been jealous every day. When we finally got into the theatre I sat eagerly anticipating a movie where a man becomes a dog but when the lights went down and yellow words moved upward across the screen "A long time ago, in a galaxy far, far away...," I quickly realized I was not going to see a canine comedy.

At first, I was angry because I had been lied to; we were about to watch some movie called *Star Wars*. Then a Star Destroyer sailed over my head, and I trembled in amazement. I'm not sure if I ever did see that Dean Jones movie but *Star Wars* blew my mind. I believe that my first viewing of the first *Star Wars* on the biggest screen in town was the beginning of my true love of film.

I remember when I began regularly attending church in my teen years and the message I felt I was getting from many church adults and leaders was "avoid the world!" Don't watch this, don't listen to that; even *Star Wars* movies were off limits. The message seemed to be, "Be afraid of the world." So, we did what most teens would do, we rebelled, just a little, and saw those movies covertly, just like most of the adults were doing. We wondered what the big deal was about seeing a movie like *Return of the Jedi* (1983), *Footloose* (1984) or *Top Gun* (1986). As teens, we were intrigued with the action, the actors and those stellar soundtracks.

I was a part of the culture around me. Culture is an interesting phenomenon. As Christians we all live within the culture around us. It's where God put us. This being so, I agree with Francis Schaeffer that in our society there are primary and secondary issues. A primary issue would be something like opposing the abhorrent practice of abortion in our nation. It is immediate and ends innocent lives which degrades the value and dignity of all human life. Secondary issues often revolve around the arts, politics, education, vocation, our regular lives. With either type of issue we by God's grace...

> ...*must exhibit both the love and the holiness of God simultaneously, so that we neither compromise the faith nor merely become hard or harsh. If that has ever been necessary for Christians, it is necessary now as we enter a real phase of*

struggle for our country and its culture. That balance of love and holiness is our first priority. (Schaeffer F. , 1982)

Watching film in an intelligent manner with the idea of engaging culture may be a secondary issue, but it is an important one. Because humans are involved. The challenge, I believe is in what L. Ryken has to say

If Christians are to be a force in shaping the contours of their society and evangelizing people in it, they will have to come to grips with the culture in which they inevitably live and move and have their being... They (Christians) will also have to know where to draw the line against becoming assimilated into a secular culture, lest they lose the quality of being separate that the Bible attributes to true believers. (Ryken, 1986)

We need to be a force in shaping and evangelizing people. We need to come to grips with our culture and not become assimilated into it. But how? This is the journey I hope to take us on. To equip us with some tools to engage our culture through an avenue that many of us share. The stuff we watch. Whether it be a movie, television show, YouTube clip or some other visual media. We need to begin to truly ENGAGE with these things in our own minds as well as with others around us. Understanding movies and how to watch them with equipped minds is an area where we can be doing that.

LAYING THE GROUNDWORK

One thing that I repeat a lot is that I want us all to remember that directors are intentionally trying to manipulate our feelings and our thoughts, among other things, and to some extent we want them to, but how do they do it?

They do it through the tools of filmmaking. When we were in our English and Literature classes at school we learned various writing essentials through reading books. There are terms like setting, character, plot, conflict and climax. There are also deeper ideas too, like allusions, motifs, symbols and themes. Movies have all those same important elements, and also have their own set of terms we need to learn, like **shot, framing, focus, angle, camera movement, sound, lighting and editing**. Learning these terms and seeing examples will help us begin to understand the groundwork of filmmaking. Rarely do any of these elements occur alone, but rather they are all used together with other tools to tell us the story in the unique way that only visual media can.

ARE YOU FILM LITERATE?

Are you a film nerd? Are you just a casual watcher? Are you a person that has been watching films all your life? Or do you mostly hang with popular films, the films that are the block-busters? Maybe you like to take on an indie film here and there and stretch your experience. Perhaps you are the person that likes to try and watch the award winning movies and nominees each year (Golden Globes, Oscars) and then afterwards wonder, "Why did that win an award?" Is it possible that you like to watch foreign films (the ones you might have to read) as well as films in black and white, and dive into various genres of film (Drama, Comedy, Horror)? Whichever way you watch, this guide will help you in dissecting any film and help you move into an understanding of its message and meaning. This is what it means to be "literate" when watching film.

If you are interested in becoming more film literate and would like a list of films to pursue I recommend checking out some of the movie lists provided by the American Film Institute (AFI). Not every movie on their list is for every person, but there are some truly great movies in their lists.

OUR FIRST QR CODE AND VIDEO CLIP

The following QR code has a fun little video that highlights, through a montage, 100 famous movie quotes from some of the most loved movies of all time according to the AFI. If you are reading this in print you can use your phone's QR reader to access the clip. Otherwise, simply click on a link

CAN'T I JUST WATCH STUFF FOR FUN?

If you are genuinely asking me that question then, no. The answer is no. Not to say watching movies won't be fun anymore, but the fun changes. Before reading the material that I present here, many of my friends and students simply watched movies or TV as a fairly brainless activity. They would casually turn something on and just as casually turn off their mind. I encourage active watching, active listening and active thinking; we need to engage with what we are watching. Some folks left their teen years thinking that learning is a chore or that it is difficult. Others are just out of practice. That saddens me. I want people to love learning; learning can be fun, especially if it is done during an activity that you already enjoy.

THE INFLUENCE OF MEDIA

...who has ever torn himself from the claw that encloses you when you [watch] TV? It grows you any shape it wishes! It is an environment as real as the world. It becomes and is the truth...with all my knowledge and skepticism, I have never

been able to argue with a [TV's} one-hundred-piece symphony orchestra, full color, [and] three dimensions...
-Faber (Bradbury, Fahrenheit 451, 1995)

What we watch shapes us. The things on the television or the screen become the "truth." Many would like to convince themselves that it isn't true, that they are not being shaped, but look at the effect media has on all those around us. In the late 1990's why did boys all over the country suddenly start to wear their pants around the low end of their bottoms? No one sent a letter or called them on the phone. They saw it on a screen and it became the norm for what was cool. As individuals, we are not immune or exempt; we are being affected as well. Just think, we sign up for cable, Netflix, Prime, and HBO. We carry smart phones everywhere now. We need to. At least, it feels that way. The rain falls on all of us. We swim in the same media swamp as everyone else.

We often hear that media is a useful tool, but what is the object of that media tool? I mean if nails are the object of a hammer, if screws are the object of a screwdriver, and wood is the object of a saw, what is the object of the media? Humans are the object, or at least our minds are. Media literally appears everywhere in our modern society: The screens in our pockets and hands, on our walls in our houses, in airports, and supermarkets, through podcasts, radio, television, ... the list is endless.

We, as believers, need to have our own tools and be equipped properly so that we can handle the ideas constantly being projected to us. Simply put, we should not hit play on a film merely to watch, listen and "veg-out." Too many people believe that movie watching is and should be a brainless activity. If we are honest, we expect to get something from a film. At the very least we want a sustained entertaining emotional moment, a sensory experience that fulfils our visual and auditory desires. Maybe we want to laugh, or cry, or feel the fear as a hero makes that fateful decision. "The best films challenge and leave us entertained, amused, uncomfortable, sometimes sad, never bored, perhaps angry." (Schaeffer F. , 1990)

Here are some examples from *Raiders of the lost Ark*, *The Matrix*, *Jaws*:

Raiders of the Lost Ark -
Indy takes back the Ark

http://tinyurl.com/yd3pj5cz

We need to admit that watching film should be an intellectual pursuit. The fact of the matter is that the creators of a movie have a purpose and a belief about things like life, ethics, and love. A created film is filled with those ideas and does not take a break from portraying its creator's agenda in full color visual and stereo sound. The writer, director, and other creators of the film had a reason for making it. The movie says those things for them every time it is viewed.

LIFELONG LEARNING

Learning is freedom, critical thinking is freedom. Having the ability to acquire new ideas and skills to question, to ponder, and to act, is freedom. Being told what to do and being unable to question either by decree (not being allowed to question) or because we don't know how, is a form of mental slavery. If a movie is affecting our thoughts and feelings, isn't it also reasonable to conclude that it is also affecting our beliefs and action?

One of the things I hope for is that people that go through this guide will never watch a film the same way again. That he or she will have a richer and more fulfilling experience by becoming an engaged watcher.

MOVIES ARE STORIES

"A movie has a story to tell and tells it with pictures, borrowing from painting, words, theatre, and music – borrowing from God." (Schaeffer F. , 1990)

It has been said, "It is not so much what the character does in the story, but what the story does in the character." I would add: **It is not as much what the story does in the character, but what the story does in the viewer**.

I think it is important to understand that those in the creative fields (like authors and directors) are intentionally trying to manipulate feelings and thoughts, influence ideologies and challenge the convictions of their viewers. They do it through stories. And we want them to!

Why do they tell stories? And why do we love stories?

Stories relate truths that are not easily defined- truths about love, fear, envy, redemption, and a character's growth. Many educated people have said that in many ways stories, even fictional ones, are more real than reality. Novelist Rich Bullock says it like this: "Fiction is truth, it just isn't true." We tell stories to connect our life experiences together with those around us. These stories can be, among other things, entertaining, humorous, serious, sad, and informative. Sometimes stories can even connect us to those who came before us and they can also prepare us for what is to come. We tell stories because we are human and the unexplainable things are what constitute, so often, the nature of humanity. We study them to connect to the writer/teller or, in the case of film, the Director, the Author or the Creator of the movie. He or she has something to tell us about life, living, and the human experience. It's a pattern we see as far back as the Bible.

> *The characteristic way of expressing religious truth in the Bible is through story, poem, vision, and letter. By comparison, expository essays, theological discourses and sermons are a relative rarity." (Ryken, 1986)*

WHAT AM I REALLY GETTING AT?

Isn't this why we study the Word of God? We need to connect with the Author, Creator and Maker; the one who fashioned humanity and understands our whole nature. We study stories because we are part of God's story. He gave us the Bible, not in the form of an instruction manual or theological treatise, but mostly in stories. God could have just given us his Ten Commandments and the laws in the Old Testament and told us, "That's it. Figure it out." But He offered so much more. He gave us true stories of Abraham and Moses, David and Hosea, Barnabas and Titus. He also told fictional stories of young men tempted by loose women, farmers sowing seed, ladies taking care of their household, and shepherds watching over their flocks. He did this for us humans who, under God's reign, struggle in our sinful humanity to become that which the Creator desires.

LAST THINGS

This guide is a survey of film techniques and is not intended as an in-depth exhaustive study of film-making. **There may be "spoilers" in some of the clips and discussions of the films referenced in this guide.** You can always look ahead and watch each film clip prior to the chapter discussion. You may also want to watch some of the films that the clips are culled from as well. I will provide a complete list of films that I used at the end of this guide book. You may also need to watch a clip more than once to see all the content there is to see. I do not pretend to know everything about all the movies and clips, but am excited to enter a discussion with you about your ideas and insights into the films we are all watching.

RECAP

- We need to change the way we watch media
- Media is a factor in shaping the way we think
- Movies are made with thought and intention; we should watch with the same deliberate purpose.
- Learning is freedom.

- Movies are stories designed to manipulate us. We look forward to this but we should be self-aware at the same time.

Unfortunately, internet links break.
If any video link above does not work,
check the link to my most updated YouTube playlist here:
OVERTURE

https://tinyurl.com/overture-chap

[3]

EXPOSITION

A COUPLE OF WALK-THROUGHS

WHAT I AM GOING TO WALK YOU THROUGH below is a window into some of the skills we all need to be familiar with when watching movies. Take a few moments and view the movie clips through the links found below. Afterwards, I am going to talk you through each clip. I am going to do most of the work in dissecting these clips. I want to show you where we are going.

If you feel so inclined, take some notes as you watch.

Some things to take note of:

- What do you see? Simply what are the things, items, characters on the screen?
- What are they doing?
- What is being said?

Try not to make judgements or force conclusions yet, just get the facts. We'll start with *Rocky*.

ROCKY (1976)

Scene Dissection (1 clip)

This is literally the opening scene in the first film of the ***Rocky*** series. In this Oscar winning film the first thing the

Rocky -
Rocky fights Spider Rico

https://tinyurl.com/ycaf5cre

audience sees is a purposeful shot of an iconographic painting of Christ. We are in a church. As the camera dollies out and downward we see our boxers. Rocky versus some dude named Spider Rico. We see trash being thrown into the ring. We understand that this is not a professional match. Rocky does not take instruction from his corner man, he is stubborn.

Now, if you didn't notice it, look back and see if you can spot what else is in the background? Below that large painting: A sign. It says "Pro Boxing" and it is blocked out by another smaller sign that says "Resurrection A.C." So, the whole sign reads "PRO BOXING, Resurrection A.C. THUR NIGHT," I doubt that this is talking about bringing the Air Conditioner back to life. Its literal meaning refers to the actual real-life building they are in, the Resurrection Athletic Club, but I also know that this tired out, lifeless, and stubborn Rocky Balboa will eventually have to fight a man named Apollo Creed (A.C.).

Let's discuss: What about that painting? Why start a movie about a down and out boxer in Philadelphia with that painting? The director picked that setting purposely. I think that it is critical and intentional that the sign appears the way that it does, under the painting of Jesus. I also know that Rocky becomes a symbol of something larger than himself. He represents the city, its people, the American Dream and somewhere in that is the theme of this film and its greatness.

HELLBOY II: The Golden Army (2008)

Scene Dissection (2 clips)

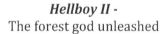

Hellboy II -
The forest god unleashed

https://tinyurl.com/yc5bp85d

Hellboy II -
Killing the forest god

https://tinyurl.com/ycna5kzn

This time you should be more aware of things to look for. So, let's look a little closer. You may have noticed that the scene takes place on a city street. There is a lot of confusion and craziness. Cars are being smashed, people are running, it's mayhem. None of this should be a surprise since there is a giant alien plant thing doing most of the damage. Did you notice that there is a movie theatre on the street where this all takes place? Did you happen to see what movie might be playing there? Watch the clip again if you need to. The theatre is on the right side of the screen. I'll wait...

Could you see what the marquee says? If not, I'll help you, "SEE YOU NEXT _ _NDAY". What might that mean? How about the neon cross up high - did you see it attached to the side of a building? It's on the left side of the screen. Did you catch the words on it? "SIN WILL FIND YOU OUT."

Now some may be saying that is no big deal, but please consider that just as an author is deliberate in what he or she puts in a novel, so are directors and writers of movies. Those two things could have easily been replaced with a soda ad or the name of an actual movie. They weren't. This is a movie set. It was built and arranged with purpose. No one said on a whim, "Hey, wouldn't it be cute to put some religious-type messages up?"

Near the end of that clip, Hellboy is poised to kill the Forest God plant with one last shot. It is at this point when he is addressed by Prince Nuada (the white-haired dude). Nuada tells Hellboy, "You could be a king." and "If you cannot command, then you must obey." Nuada and Hellboy are standing atop a high place when all this happens. I want to pair something up alongside this section. I can't help but think there is a reference to a more important work of writing, an allusion, in the conversation and the placement of these two characters in this scene. Take a moment to read Matthew 4: 8-11:

> *Again, the Devil took Him to a very high mountain and showed Him all the kingdoms of the world and their glory; and he said to Him, "All these things I will give You, if You fall down and worship me." Then Jesus said to him, "Go, Satan! For it is written, 'You shall worship the Lord your God, and serve Him only.'" Then the devil left Him." (ESV, 2001)*

Is there an ironic parallel in this scene to that verse?

My purpose here is not to tell you what to think but rather as we watch, to encourage us to be thinking, even if we are simply watching a comic book movie. Speaking of comic book movies...

SPIDERMAN 2 (2004)

Scene dissection (2 clips)

Spiderman 2 -
The train battle

https://tinyurl.com/y8rckedh

Spiderman 2 -
Stopping the train

https://tinyurl.com/y9stxbyy

In these scenes, there is a fight between two characters. One character seems willing to sacrifice his life for others. The other man does not care about people.

As the hero, Spiderman puts himself between the danger and the people on the train. Did you notice the position of Spiderman's body as he places himself on the front of the train? One cannot discount the symbol of a cross he makes as he slings his webs. The body in the shape of a cross is quite common in film, but it is always purposeful. The director is using it for a reason, but there is something more in this clip. After he gives everything and begins to fall, Peter Parker/Spiderman is taken in by the passengers. Just as **Hellboy 2** has deeper ideas, the scene in **Spiderman 2** also appears to be alluding to something.

Here are a few examples of what I am talking about:

Botticelli

https://tinyurl.com/y8otmvqj

Caravaggio

https://tinyurl.com/y894q6hp

Raphael

https://tinyurl.com/raphaeldeposition

Did you see it?

The first link is to Botticelli's *Lamentation Over the Dead Christ*. The second is Caravaggio's *The Entombment of Christ* and the third is Raphael's *Deposition of Christ*. What is the significance to the position of Spiderman's body as he saves those people on the train and again with the position of his body in relation to those paintings and other paintings like it?

WRAP-UP

Being purposeful in analyzing film is only the first step, but it's an important one that leads to some bigger questions. What does it mean to be a force in shaping the contours of our society? Or to be a force in evangelizing our community? How do we come to grips with our culture? I think that visual media, especially films, is an avenue we can be utilizing to connect to our culture. As believers, we need to be equipped to critically view and wisely employ our skills in watching movies to talk with those around us. It is in these discussions that we can connect, care and eventually share the hope and love that is found in Christ Jesus. That is what I want to equip you to do.

So how do I get you there? How do I get you the tools and the skills to watch a film and recognize the symbols, motifs and messages of these writers and directors?

This guide will now turn its focus to what I call the grammar of film: The building blocks of movies, the techniques, lingo, and other tools used in their creation. When we begin to understand how moviemakers make films we can start considering how they convey their messages. We will begin by looking at individual movie components including sound, camera angle, the shot, and lighting. As usual, I will include relevant examples and film clips along the way.

RECAP

- Movies are complex ways of telling the moviemaker's view of the world.
- Their complexity is designed and purposeful.
- Sometimes the intricate design of a scene can hide things that are rather obvious.
- If we are watching film and media, we should be using it to engage our culture.

Unfortunately, internet links break. If any video link above does not work, check the link to my most updated YouTube playlist here:
EXPOSITION

https://tinyurl.com/exposition-chap

[4]

THE SHOT AND CAMERA ANGLES

THE SHOT

THERE IS AN EXERCISE that I often have participants of my film classes do. I tell them to take a sheet of paper and roll it into a tube. Imagine that the tube is now like looking through the lens of a camera. Peering through it, you see a shot. Each time you open your eyes it is a new shot. Each time you blink you end the shot. You can do all sorts of things that a camera does. You can pan across a room, you can track by walking, you can move close or move farther away. This is what a camera does.

The shot is an uninterrupted span of time and it is the basic element that all films are built on. All the shots of a film are edited together in a particular sequence in order to build a complete film. The shot is also a general term which has different aspects that we need to understand because there are many different types of shots that directors can use. Some of the more popular terms are the **Long Shot,**

Medium Shot, and Close Shot. Each of these has a different effect on the viewer.

Below is a short video that gives examples of various types of shots that directors use. As you watch the video I want you to consider what each kind of shot makes you think about or feel. Pay attention to how the change in the distance of the lens from the subject changes how you think. What about the angle? What might a director accomplish with certain shots?

Basic Camera Shots/Angles

http://tinyurl.com/yb7hjbo6

BASIC CAMERA SHOTS:

By having a basic understanding of the shot, we can now see that a director must make purposeful choices in the shots he or she will use to shoot a scene. A scene is simply a set of shots that have been edited together in a particular order. I do not plan on addressing every type of shot used in filmmaking. Instead, I will point out a few specific types of shots.

THE ESTABLISHING SHOT

Oftentimes a director will give what is called an Establishing Shot, which is supposed to tell the viewer where the action of a scene takes place. It is used to create setting. The establishing shot can be a sweeping shot across a forest land, flying over a well-known city or simply show the front of a building. For instance, if there is a still shot of an exterior of a stadium, then the next shot is of a character inside a room, we as the audience will assume the character is inside that same structure. This type of shot and editing happens all the time, and we expect it.

ESTABLISHING SHOT EXAMPLE:

In this example, we are shown the exterior of Yankee Stadium and then immediately the next shot is in an office. The idea, of course, is that the office and characters are inside of that baseball stadium. Because our brains fill in

Seinfeld -
Establishing shot

http://tinyurl.com/y94tef2m

gaps and because we have been trained through having seen this happen before, we do not need to be told this information. We are not confused. For us, the audience, it is seamless, even though these characters could be (and probably are) sitting in a sound stage in California. We believe that they are in New York, inside Yankee Stadium.

Camera Angles:

What can angle do for us? Let's look at a clip from a classic film that is often at the top of must-watch film lists, directed by Orson Welles. Notice how he uses a drastic angle to affect his audience.

- How do the characters appear when shot from this low angle?
- What feeling do you think that the director is trying to achieve from this scene?

Many would claim that this angle makes the characters

Citizen Kane -
Low angle

http://tinyurl.com/ybpfxrmr

appear dominant and strong, larger than life. It also makes things appear intense and serious.

The film **Citizen Kane** broke a lot of rules for its time and many people did not understand or appreciate the techniques that Orson Welles used in making it. Imagine you are in 1941, in a theatre audience about to watch this film. Most films of that time were filmed with simple shots (mid, long, close-up) and basic camera angles (single shot, two-shot, over the shoulder). Instead, you're watching a film where the camera is down by the actors' feet. How do you think you might have reacted to this change from your movie-watching expectations?

There are many other interesting stories about the making of this film, including the use of the wide-angle lens, deep-focus, the use of ceilings in a film and the fact that to get that low angle shot Welles had to cut holes in the stage floor big enough to fit the camera and its crew inside. We will experience this film a few more times in clips throughout this guide.

Next in the world of camera angles we are going to look at the iconic thriller **Psycho** (1960) by Alfred Hitchcock.

Watch the two scenes of Norman talking with the beautiful Marion. The dialogue is great, but I want you to particularly pay attention to the camera angles.

- How do the characters appear when shot from various angles?
- How do the camera angles affect the mood of the scene?
- Did your feelings towards the characters change during either scene? Why?
- What feeling do you think that the director is trying to achieve from this scene?

First, we see both characters in a mid or medium shot. The camera sits basically in front looking at the characters.

Did you notice how Norman keeps looking up and off to his right? He acts as if his mom can hear him. Then suddenly Norman's camera angle changes; the camera is closer and below him looking up. How does this change the temper of their conversation? And what about that stuffed owl now hanging over him, watching him? Then in the next scene the camera is much closer to his face and he leans into it. How does this change how we feel? Should Marion be concerned? Do we now think there is something a little "off" with Norman Bates?

Just as the low angle shot in **Citizen Kane** creates a certain effect and feeling, an extreme high angle shot can do this as well. Extreme angles can also be a little deceptive. Here is a high angle shot from **Psycho.**

We start the scene from a low angle as Norman passes us and walks up the stairs. Then the camera moves by crane

Psycho -
Norman argues with mother

https://tinyurl.com/y8hl3x68

forward and up the stairs as we begin to hear a heated discussion. The camera continues upward until it is peering straight down over the doorway of the bedroom and the stairs. Then we see Norman carrying his mother out of the bedroom and down the stairs.

- What effect do the high camera angles have on the scene?
- How is it different from the low angle? How do the characters appear?
- If you have seen the film Psycho in its entirety you must know what deception is happening in this scene. This deception genuinely tightens the suspense for those that are new to the film. Why?

Camera angles are important to a film and the mood that a director is trying to achieve. They can add mystery or create an uneasy feeling. They can show characters as superior or simply mess with our perception. Pay attention to how a director uses camera angles to enhance the emotional tone of a scene.

RECAP

- The Shot is the basic element of every film.
- There are many types of shots.
- The Establishing Shot is often how directors create setting.
- Camera angles can create tension and affect how we think about a character, among other things.

Unfortunately, internet links break. If any video link
above does not work, check the link to my most updated
YouTube playlist here:
The SHOT and CAMERA ANGLES

https://tinyurl.com/shot-camang-chapt

[5]

FOCUS

SPEAKING OF MESSING WITH OUR PERCEPTION, there is the subtle art of focus. Directors love to use the focus of the camera lens not just to direct a movie, but to direct our attention as audience members within the scene and on the screen. The most obvious concept about focus is the crispness or clarity of the subjects in the shot, whether this is scenery or characters or furniture.

You may think "Of course everything will be in focus. It would be annoying or wrong for a director to blur an image." Watch this scene from *Young Victoria* (2009). Pay attention to how the director directs your eyes around the screen, not by moving the camera but by adjusting the focus. It is called Rack Focusing.

Young Victoria
A dinner party

https://tinyurl.com/ya4yve3x

Another focusing technique that directors use is the soft focus. Soft-focus is when a director will ever so slightly blur a shot either of one character or a whole scene. Notice in the following scene from *Casablanca* (1942) the difference between the type of focus used on Rick and how it is not the same as the type of focus used on Ilsa.

- Why would a director use the soft-focus lens?
- What effect are we supposed to get from its use?

Casablanca
Rick and Ilsa

https://tinyurl.com/ybdgac2f

- Imagine a whole scene in soft focus, what might a soft-focus scene mean?

Another technique that Orson Welles used in ***Citizen Kane*** was a deep-focus lens. A deep-focus lens allows the whole shot to be in focus at the same time. This means that the background and the foreground are all crisp. It allows the person watching to look anywhere on the screen with ease.

That last clip shows the use of the deep focus technique where the viewer can see everything in focus. All things in

Citizen Kane
You buy a bag of peanuts

https://tinyurl.com/y9kr93jo

the foreground and the background can be clearly seen, even the chorus girls who don't seem to know the words to the song they are lip-synching.

- Why would a director use the deep-focus technique?
- What effect are we supposed to get from its use?

In this next clip, a director purposely makes the audience deal with focus. It is obvious. The scene is from ***Deconstructing Henry*** (1997) where Woody Allen intentionally and specifically blurs out just one character. He is obviously using focus to make a statement about that character's situation in life. If we can't figure out why the character is blurry, the characters themselves attempt to tell us what it might mean. Perhaps he is a symbol or a recurring motif.

Various focusing techniques are often covert ways that directors control the visual aspect of the film that the audience is watching.

Deconstructing Henry
Mel's out of focus

https://tinyurl.com/yawlh6be

RECAP

- How a director uses focus in a scene is intentional and manipulative.
- The use of rack focus can move our eyes to various places on the screen without changing the shot.
- Soft focus can create a sympathetic feeling or tone.
- Deep focus can allow a director to put everything on the screen or in the scene at once.
- Directors sometimes challenge their audience overtly.

Unfortunately, internet links break. If any video link
above does not work, check the link to my most
updated YouTube playlist here:

FOCUS

https://tinyurl.com/focus-chapt

[6]

CAMERA MOVEMENT

THE CAMERA MOVES. I am sure that this is not new information, but how the camera moves is something we should be aware of. I believe that most of the time we as audience members don't realize how much work the camera is doing.

Some basic camera moves are the Pan (panoramic), Tilt, Dolly, Zoom, and the use of a Vest. All these, plus many others, are all ways a director controls the content of each shot. Camera movement can affect the emotion of a scene, the pace of the film and can also create surprise by either hiding or revealing elements just outside what the viewer can see.

THE BASICS

In the following scene from **Wyatt Earp** (1994) there are many camera movement techniques. I suggest watching the clip once without sound so that you have an easier time taking note of these camera movements. Again, think back to my earlier illustration of using a rolled-up tube as your lens.

Things to look for:

- **Pan**: Camera turns to the side on a horizontal axis like you would turn your head.
- **Tilt**: Camera tilts on vertical axis, up and down as in looking up or down.
- **Tracking**: The camera moves along with the characters. A dolly shot will often use tracks like a little train might use. Similar shots are called truck, dolly.
- **Crane**: The camera is attached to a crane that allows the camera to move around a character up into the air and down to the ground. Also called boom shot.
- **Drone**: Today a camera is often attached to a flying drone that can accomplish some of these types of shots and even more.

In this scene there are about 70 different shots edited

Wyatt Earp
Gunfight at the O.K. Corral

https://tinyurl.com/yaxxqq9o

together where we see all sorts of camera movement. There are a few pans. One is of the group of men from the front. We see each face as the camera moves slowly to the left.

The dolly or tracking shots are when the camera moves alongside the men as they walk down the street. There is a tilt as we see their boots walking in the dust, then the camera angles up to show us their faces from a low angle. The crane shot happens when the camera starts off in front of the characters and then rises up high, swings around and tilts down behind the group. There is another crane shot when a character walks into the shot; the camera starts from a high angle and it drops down in front of his face.

WEARING THE CAMERA

The next clips use a technique accomplished by attaching a camera to an operator with a vest system. A worn system allows the camera to go wherever the subject goes. The camera operator can run, walk, go around, or otherwise move around with the shot. One type of worn camera system is called a Steadicam. This allows a camera to move and track with a more fluid and smoother look. It has less jiggle and jarring than a camera simply held by hands.

Rocky
Running the stairs 1

https://tinyurl.com/rockrunstair1

Rocky
Running the stairs 2

https://tinyurl.com/y7sb2xxf

We return to **Rocky** for the Steadicam shot. Once again try watching each clip without sound the first time, and then again with sound. I am asking you to do this to focus on what the camera is doing. How does it move? Is it stationary and then it begins moving? If it moves then stops, where and when does it do that? Pay attention to the camera's movement.

These are obviously two parallel scenes from **Rocky**. I wanted to put those two similar running scenes next to each other in your mind because when people talk about **Rocky** and the greatness of the movie we rarely remember that first clip. We usually only recall the second one. They both show Rocky running those stairs, but if you are attentive you will see that there is a little more going on. Let me tell you a little about how the camera's movement is telling the audience something.

In the first scene, it is dark. Rocky is training. He gets to those famous steps but he is barely making it. The camera is at the bottom of the steps when Rocky begins to go up. He starts to hold his side.

- What is the camera doing?
- Is it keeping up with him?
- Is he even going to make it?
- Why does the camera stop going up the stairs?

In the second clip, it is still early morning but it is lighter outside. Rocky has more energy, he seems driven. The camera appears to be moving quite fast along the docks. He has a renewed sense of purpose. We are at the steps. He appears near the bottom and is coming up. But where is the camera this time? Not at the bottom. The camera is up the steps a little way, waiting for him. What might this mean? He reaches the step that the camera is on and then it continues with him the rest of the way. Even without the sound we should get it. It is as if the camera was waiting where it left him the last time he went up those steps, as if the camera, like us, was hoping he would come back.

Our discussion about sound is coming up, but if you watch these clips again with sound it is obvious that the first clip has some sparse music. It might sound a little dreary and that is exactly how the clip plays out. The second clip is the one that everyone knows, with the famous song "Gonna Fly Now" playing. It is hopeful and exciting, and the reason why everyone who sees the film wants to run those steps in Philadelphia. It is actually the layering of those two clips and other contrasting scenes that give the film much of its depth and richness.

ZOOM VERSUS DOLLY

I listed zoom as a camera movement, but it is sort of a fake camera move. The camera is not technically moving in a zoom, although it may appear as if there is movement. All that is really happening is that a camera lens is being adjusted or turned to magnify or compress what is seen. It directs our attention, emphasizing what is on the screen.

A dolly shot, in contrast, is where the camera actually moves in towards the subject or moves out and away. A dolly shot and zoom shot can sometimes be confused.

Vertigo
In the museum

https://tinyurl.com/ycpxmmjr

In this clip, we start with an establishing shot that we are to assume is the art museum in which our character is in the next shot. As our character walks around the museum he sees a woman. We see the woman. What is the man looking at? Zoom, ah that's what he sees. What else does he see? Zoom again. The director is telling us exactly what he wants us to know and the character hasn't even said a word.

- What do you think Hitchcock want us to see? To feel? Believe?
- What is he telling us about the man?
- What is he telling us about the woman?

This next scene shows us a dolly shot. Notice how the camera slowly pushes in on Al Pacino's character, Michael. This is not a zoom.

The Godfather
Strictly business

https://tinyurl.com/y7qepzmv

- How does this effect make us feel about the character?
- How about what he is saying?
- How is this different than the zoom?

THE VERTIGO EFFECT

Sometimes a director likes to mess with the audience and create some special moments that challenge our perceptions. In the following scene, we see the Vertigo Effect. What does this shot tell us about the character?

Vertigo
The bell tower

https://tinyurl.com/y834j4oy

Hitchcock accomplished this technique by manipulating the zoom and dollying the camera at the same time. He also suspended the camera in midair.

- What affect does it create in the viewer?
- Why does the director choose to do this?

This effect has been used in many other films since. In fact, we'll see this again in the Intermission.

THE DRONE SHOT

In this next scene, we are watching a camera shot from a drone as Bond comes out of the balcony doorway.

Spectre
To death

https://tinyurl.com/y8jzewz2

This shot would have been much more difficult using cranes, dollies and/or a helicopter considering where the character is on top of a building, and the varied terrain he walks across.

THE SHAKY CAM

The next camera movement technique we will address is the shaky cam. It has become quite popular in action movies. Essentially the camera never stops moving. It often might feel as if the camera has a mind of its own.

The Bourne Ultimatum
Opening scene

https://tinyurl.com/yd8ylhcn

- What affect does the shaky camera have?
- How does the shakiness of the camera change throughout the scene?
- What causes it to change?
- What are the out of focus or streaked scenes about? How did you figure this out?

Even though the movement appears out of control and random, notice how it is always on target. It never loses its subject and is almost intuitive in how it gets everything in the scene that it is supposed to.

REVEALING WHAT IS HIDDEN

Oftentimes camera movement is intentionally directing our attention to specific things. This might be to give information but it also may be intended to hide things that are off-screen. Remember that even though a novel might be able to explain to us in words what is going on in a character's mind a film cannot easily do this. This must be done through various means like facial expression, camera movement, and sound. In the next clip from **Atonement** we are watching the face of a soldier. He sees something. He needs to get a closer look. He does not appear happy. What is it?

Atonement
Girls in a field

https://tinyurl.com/y849fn4w

- What is the effect that the slow reveal has on us as an audience?
- Notice that we get to see his reaction as the secret is revealed.
- How does it make us feel?

CHARACTER POV

Every so often the camera becomes the character, or at least the eyes of the character. For many this is called a Point of View Shot or POV. In this next scene from *The Sixth Sense* (1999), Bruce Willis is Dr. Malcolm Crowe and he is playing a "mind reading game" with Cole in an attempt to communicate with the child. The game is to have Cole step forward for each guess Malcolm gets right and to take a step back for each wrong guess. Pay attention to what the camera does on the wrong answers.

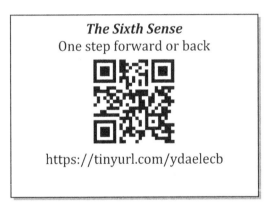

The Sixth Sense
One step forward or back

https://tinyurl.com/ydaelecb

- Why does the director choose to use the camera as the eyes of the boy?
- Which character does it makes us focus on more?

THE UNMOTIVATED CAMERA

Usually, camera movement is motivated by on screen clues, like character movement or the action of the visual elements on screen. Sometimes a director moves a camera in a way that does not seem to coincide with the action on the screen. It is as if the camera gets a mind of its own. This type of movement is called Unmotivated Camera Movement and can have a meaning in and of itself. This next scene is from *Children of Men* (2006).

Children of Men
Café bomb blast

https://tinyurl.com/y9hz6wpk

- What was the camera thinking as Clive Owen's character walked out of the coffee shop?
- How does it make you feel when the camera simply moves away from the action or the character on screen?
- How does the camera's unmotivated action affect our motivation?

It should be quite apparent that camera movement is a complex and essential part of making a film. Directors are purposeful in choosing how the camera will shoot a scene, whether it is stationary or if it should move. Each choice will add to the meaning of the film's message and how it will affect us in the audience.

THE EXTENDED SHOT

The next camera movement can also be called a long take. The extended shot is where the shot lasts for an extended time. In other words, there are no cuts and no edits. It is like not blinking. The long shot is unique because everything must be preplanned. Everything. All action, dialogue and movement of the camera must be preplanned and choreographed with all other movement in and around the scene being shot.

Following is the first shot from *Gravity*. The original shot is actually longer than 15 minutes. This is a short section from it.

This next scene is once again from the innovative Orson Welles' *Citizen Kane*. This is an extended shot that goes

Gravity
Opening scene

https://tinyurl.com/yajyhqwm

through rooms and around furniture and other obstacles. Speaking of furniture, how does that table get in there?

This shot is special because of the bulk of the equipment at the time. Welles didn't have vest systems and small cameras that could be hand-held. He didn't have computers

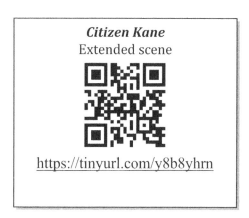

Citizen Kane
Extended scene

https://tinyurl.com/y8b8yhrn

and green screens. This shot was done the old-fashioned way, with innovation and hard work. Don't forget the use of that deep focus which allows us to see young Charles Kane playing in the snow outside the same time there is dialogue inside.

The third scene is from the opening scene in *La La Land.*

La La Land
Opening scene

https://tinyurl.com/yb6k525e

- What sort of affect does this type of shot create?
- What sorts of things would have to be figured out beforehand?
- Why would a director do an extended shot?

There is in fact a film that was shot entirely in one take. It is called ***Russian Ark*** (2002). It runs almost 100 minutes and has no cuts.

RECAP

- It is important for us to understand how much work the

Russian Ark
Trailer

https://tinyurl.com/ybjldef2

camera is doing.

- There are some common camera movements like panning, tilting and tracking.
- Wearing the camera allows the camera to move with the actor
    o A Steadicam has a smoother feel.
- Sometimes a director controls what we see by zooming the camera lens in or out and not moving the camera.
    o A director may also choose to move a camera closer or farther on a dolly.
- When a director chooses to do both simultaneously, we get what is called the Vertigo Effect.
- Drones have become a useful tool in getting great shots
- Camera movement in the sense of always moving has become known as the "shaky cam" shot.
- Even though the camera shows us what is happening, it can also be used to hide what is happening and keep it from us creating tension.
- The camera often will become the eyes of the character and we will see things as the character sees it.
- An unmotivated camera is one where the camera seems to do its own thing and not follow the actions or central figure on the screen.
- Finally, the movement of the camera is indispensable when a director is trying to capture an extended shot and not cut a scene for a long time.

Unfortunately, internet links break. If any video link above does not work, check the link to my most updated YouTube playlist here:

CAMERA MOVEMENT

https://tinyurl.com/cam-move-chapt

[7]

SOUND

PEOPLE WANT TO HEAR SOMETHING when they are watching a film. Even in old silent films, sound was essential and a live orchestra would often be playing along with the film. Today there are sophisticated sound systems in movie theatres and in our homes. And because of this, directors use sounds like music, dialogue, various noises, and even silence to their advantage in creating a scene.

When talking about sound there is a term we must understand: **Diegetic Sound**. Diegetic sounds are sounds that can be logically heard by the characters in the film. So, if a character walks through a door and it creaks, she hears the creak of the door. There are also non-diegetic sounds which are sounds that the audience hears but the characters do not, like the soundtrack. Then there is the term internal-diegetic that describes sounds inside a character's head, often from a memory or flashback, like the voices Jason Bourne heard in one of our previous clips.

The next scenes will focus on sound. We have already seen how sound can affect us through those running scenes from **Rocky**. Let's look at a few other clips.

In this first clip, how does sound affect the characters in the movie and the audience watching. If you had been in the original audience when **Jurassic Park** came out, this scene had quite an impact on the audience. In fact, a new sound system had been created just for films like this. It took surround sound to a whole new level.

Jurassic Park
Meeting tyrannosaurus

https://tinyurl.com/yce8kr77

What are the sounds we hear in this clip? Rain and thunder, the snapping of the wires, and eventually the roar of a T-Rex. How about the kids breathing and screaming? How does that add to the tension of the scene? Notice that there is no soundtrack or music being used in the scene.

Here is a crucial scene in **Star Wars IV**. Notice all the sounds used in it.

Star Wars IV
Kenobi vs. Vader

https://tinyurl.com/yb4p8lbf

How important are sounds for a film like **Star Wars**? There were a lot of sounds that had to be created just for this film: Darth Vader's breathing, Light Sabers, R2D2, Laser Guns, Explosions, and even the sounds of the spaceship, the Millennium Falcon.

How is sound used in this next scene from **Road to Perdition**?

Road to Perdition
I'm glad it's you

https://tinyurl.com/ybnoacrk

- The director intentionally messes with the sound of the scene. Why?

- What is the effect of having only a slow sad tune of strings and piano playing?
- Why does the diegetic sound return when it does?
- What do you understand about the two men at the end of the scene?
- Why do we hear the gun at the end but we didn't hear it during the gun battle?

This next clip uses a little more than sound. What is it?

Open Range
No varmints or vagrants

https://tinyurl.com/yb9s7qug

- What happens to the camera when Charley Waite shoots the sign with the shogun?
- What affect does this have?

We know that sound is integral to the overall impact of a film, from the sounds characters can hear in their environment and in their head (diegetic) as well as what only we can hear as an audience (non-diegetic).

THEME MUSIC

Theme music is so integral to so many films it can become, in a sense, a character of its own. Below are videos of just the orchestra playing the theme from three well-known films. The clips I have chosen only show the orchestra that is playing the music. If you play them while closing your eyes you can probably envision a scene from the film. Notice how different the composition seems when the associated visuals from the film are not there to support the ideas in our minds.

Most of us, even if we never saw the film, can't listen to that music without thinking of open ocean water and a great white shark as large as a boat lurking underneath looking for some unsuspecting dangling legs begging to be chomped by those sharp, white, teeth.

Again, this next song is hard to hear without thinking of Norman Bates and that shower scene that was, and still is, so shocking, especially if you move the time forward on the

Jaws
Theme song

https://tinyurl.com/yaoxlbm7

video to approximately 5:50, the shower scene.

Finally, I offer a split screen of this famous song. It is

from a movie that is affectionately termed a spaghetti western, mainly because it was filmed in Italy and not where it was set, which is in the Southwestern United States. Here we can see not only the orchestra playing and the beautiful Susanna Rigacci singing, we get to see the scene from the movie where this music appears. Give it about ten seconds. I must admit that even after hearing this song many times, her voice can still give me chills.

The Good, the Bad, the Ugly
"The Ecstasy of Gold"

https://tinyurl.com/y9jlpglw

RECAP

- Diegetic sound is the sound that can be heard logically in a setting (a car driving by in the street).
  - o Non-diegetic sounds are all the sounds we may hear as an audience but the character could not hear them in their setting (theme music building).
- Sounds have an effect on the audience creating tension, excitement, and all sorts of other feelings.
- The music of a movie is also important, especially theme music.
- Many times, a film can be identified by its theme music.

Unfortunately, internet links break. If any video link above does not work, check the link to my most updated YouTube playlist here:

SOUND

https://tinyurl.com/sound-chapt

[8]

LIGHTING

LIGHT ALLOWS US TO see a film on a screen as it comes through the projector and out into the theatre. It splashes the film onto the screen and is reflected into our own eyes. Light quite literally brings life to a television screen. Light is the absence of dark but it also allows us to recognize the dark. The contrast of light, whether sharp or subtle, shapes our perception of what we see. Light is critical to the cinematography of any film.

Most films use a standard **3-point lighting system**. This system of lighting uses a **Key Light** as the main light on the front of the subject. The second light is a **Fill Light** which is usually located to the side of the subject. Lastly, there is a **Back Light** that helps to push the subject out away from the background. This lighting system will often perfectly light an actor's face. It is a great lighting technique in scenes full of light but it does not lend itself well to other applications.

Our first clip in this chapter is from *It's a Wonderful Life*. The scene takes place outside on a fairly overcast night, yet notice how well each actor's face is lit.

It's A Wonderful Life
Lasso the moon

https://tinyurl.com/y7yk2jxu

The scene and faces are generally well lit but does it feel natural? Would people outside on an overcast night with no streetlights or other lights be so well lit? We usually accept lighting like this simply because we can see the characters clearly.

In old television shows and films lighting could be challenging, sometimes the filmmakers would shoot an outdoor night scene at noon and put a dark filter over the lens. Noon would help with any long shadows but would still allow the actors to be lit.

Then there is **Practical Lighting**. The practical lighting technique is where a director appears to be using the lights that occur naturally to light the characters or the scene. For instance, here is a scene using practical lighting from *The Killing* (1956).

The Killing
The plan

https://tinyurl.com/y8qop6wm

There appears to be only one real light in the room. It is hung in the middle of the group and just above their heads. The darkness outside the circle is real. Only the front of each man is lit and if they sit back they almost disappear.

Lighting Used as a Motif or Message

Here are a couple of scenes from *Million Dollar Baby* (2004). Notice the lighting of the characters. Here the lighting design may be communicating more than what is being   said.

Million Dollar Baby
Maggie and Dupris

https://tinyurl.com/yblw7z6g

Million Dollar Baby
Maggie and Frank

https://tinyurl.com/y7docwqt

You may have noticed that these two scenes are quite similar. (Ironically the last parallel scenes I chose were also from a movie about boxing).

- What is the director trying to achieve by using such stark lighting techniques?
- What might the fact that most character's faces are usually half lit tell us about each character?
- Why do both Dupris and Frank start half in the darkness and then walk out?

Now sit back and take in this next scene. There is a robbery about to take place and the characters you see are bad guys. They work in the dark. This is practical lighting at its best.

Notice the lanterns, that train light coming around the

The Assassination of Jesse James by the Coward Howard Ford
Robbing the train

https://tinyurl.com/y8s2or8e

bend and the hiders in the woods. The sparks from the steel. The steam. It is almost magical.

Did you catch the camera movement when the front of the train catches the stationary camera and it tracks with it?

RECAP

- The 3-point lighting system is the industry standard but directors cannot be limited to this idea.
- Many films also utilize practical lighting or lighting that looks like it should if it were a real setting.
- Lighting tells us many things by what it shows and what it doesn't, much like the camera.
- Lighting can also be used to create a motif or message.

Unfortunately, internet links break. If any video link above does not work, check the link to my most updated YouTube playlist here:

LIGHTING

https://tinyurl.com/chapter-lighting

[9]

INTERMISSION

I AM HOPING that you have started to see some basic changes in the way you watch. I have taken you very quickly through some of the most basic techniques in making movies. I call it the grammar of movies. Perhaps you have begun to notice the camera angles or camera movement in the last movie you saw. How about the lighting and sound? It is difficult to parse out one aspect of filmmaking because all the scenes we have seen have multiple technical elements woven throughout them even though we tried to emphasize one thing at a time. If we looked at a whole film, all the elements we have discussed so far and so many more are at work continuously.

Our next step is to look for all these various elements at work at the same time. Feel free to go back and look at any of the clips from the previous chapters. Look back and see how **Rocky** uses lighting or how **Road to Perdition** uses camera movement.

I also thought it would be fun to throw in a few new clips that we haven't seen yet and look at what they have to offer. Pay attention to the numerous elements we have discussed: The **Shot, Angles, Movement, Focus, Sound,** and **Lighting**.

My hope is that now you have some things to start talking about as you watch a film. These are basic elements to be sure but you should be able to begin seeing how filmmakers use these things to tell their story in a unique way.

This next clip is from *Jaws*. Sheriff Brody is trying to relax by the beach but he is well aware that there is a threat in that water somewhere. One of the sheriff's biggest problems, his flaw, is that he doesn't like the water.

This scene is supposed to create some anxiety and some fear in us. Does it? How did that happen? No one came in with a deep threatening voice and said, "You need to be scared now."

Notice how the scene does not start off scary. The

Jaws
Bad hat Harry

https://tinyurl.com/ybkb9mhl

beginning is almost humorous. We attribute Sheriff Brody's anxiousness to simple personal worry. No one else seems concerned.

Are you concerned? Or are you like one of the people on the beach?

How do we take a clip like this one and deal with it?

We do it by utilizing the tools we have been talking about so far. The different shots and angles, the sounds and the music, the camera movement and focus.

Now let's look at another scene. This scene is from the opening scene of an old Orson Welles film called *A Touch of Evil*; right away we know from the title that there will be some suspense. Sure enough, look at how the clip starts. Doesn't that thing look like a bomb?

Hopefully with this shot you took notice of the **Camera Movement.**

A Touch of Evil
Opening scene

https://tinyurl.com/yb43y3wp

- Who exactly are we supposed to be watching during this scene?
- Are we watching the couple in the car?
- The car with a bomb in the trunk? Or are we watching the couple that is walking?
- Does the camera operator know what's going on?
- Who is important?

It seems there is a mystery and suspense to it. Before I move on to the next clip, did you notice anything else about this scene from the film? It was done in one extended shot.

In this next scene, we have three characters in a discussion.

- What are they talking about?
- I mean what are they really talking about?

Notice how the scene builds.

In the beginning, all the shots seem fairly innocuous. Pay attention to how Father Flynn is shot just below mid-level. We are looking ever so slightly up at him. He is standing and the ladies are sitting. Notice that in the side-shot

Doubt
Discussing Donald Miller

https://tinyurl.com/y7hk57up

towards Meryl Streep's character, Sister Beauvier, he seems larger than her in the background. What point of view, or views, are we seeing this scene in? His or theirs?

Suddenly, the conversation shifts. Philip Seymore Hoffman's Father Flynn asks, "Did you want to discuss the pageant? Is that why I am here or is this what you wanted to discuss?" It is at this point that there is a change in the camera on Meryl Streep. Is it mid-level? Low angle? Nope. Look at how the shot changes when she is shown saying, "This." Notice she doesn't say it right away. Then that phone. Did you feel the palpable unease in the room?

From there, the camera angle changes to Dutch when it shows the phone. What is the effect of this new angle? What happens to the angle and the feeling tone as the scene moves on? Consider Sister Beauvier's relentless pursuit or Father Flynn's explanation? By the end of the scene, do you doubt?

This ends our intermission. Except to remind you that this is really just the beginning. I am excited to discuss a complex movie making technique that can radically alter not just a scene but everything in a movie, including the acting. This technique is the Editing.

RECAP

- We have only brushed the surface of film making techniques but hopefully you now know a little more about how moviemakers do their work and how it affects us.

- Now we need to put it all together looking at all the ideas we have discussed.

- Feel free to go back and look at some of the clips outside of the chapters they were used.
    - For instance, check out the lighting techniques in **Road to Perdition** and the camera angles and sound in **Million Dollar Baby.**

- Look once more at the **Rocky**, **Hellboy II** and **Spiderman 2** clips from chapter 3, Exposition that I walked you through. You should be able to see the techniques and appreciate these on a deeper level.

Unfortunately, internet links break. If any video link above does not work, check the link to my most updated YouTube playlist here:

INTERMISSION

https://tinyurl.com/chapter-intermission

[10]

EDITING

The Art of Editing
by Tom Waldek

https://tinyurl.com/ybjb2p65

EDITING INVOLVES THE ASSEMBLING of all the various shots of the film done by the director into a cohesive whole. Editing is an art. What makes it an art is that most editors will tell you that they edit by feeling and sense and not by any hard and fast rules. When to cut, what to assemble and in which order are all personal preferences, a matter of artistic vision and not industry formula. Basically, editing in its most rudimentary concept is the ability to show the audience a shot, then cut from that shot, and connect to a new shot over and over. It sounds so simple. In fact, all movies are an assemblage or a montage of shots (unless of course the movie was done with one shot).

Even though editing is very complex and there are no real instruction manuals about when and what to cut, there are some common editing terms and general rules we can learn that will help us understand some of the basic ideas that go into editing. We have already experienced most of these techniques in the clips we have watched.

I feel the best way to understand these terms is to see them in use so watch this next clip and I will attempt to explain some.

- **Cutting on action**- This means that an editor wants to cut as the action is happening and matches any

Harry and the Hendersons
The Dumpster

https://tinyurl.com/y7jwrrbo

  movement that is occurring. Watch all the quick cuts that occur as the man with a rifle walks in front of the dump truck.
- **Match cut** – This is matching one cut with the next. As the man moves in front of the truck all the cuts match.

In other words, his actions seem fluid as if it were one continuous shot.

- **Cross-cutting** (Parallel cut)- placing connected shots of two events happening at different places within each other so the feel is that they are happening simultaneously. This is when the rifle falls out of the dumpster and we see another man running. We assume he has been running while the dumpster scene is happening at the same time.

- **Eye-line match**- Inside the dumpster the shots go back and forth between the monster and the man with a gun. Their eyes are at similar heights so we feel that they are looking at each other.

- **Cutaway**- Anytime that that camera cuts away from the main action. Like when the rifle flies out of the dumpster and we see it hit the ground. Or when the man crossing in front of the truck looks up and we see a quick shot of just the dumpster above his head. This can also be an insert shot.

- **Insert** – This shot is often a close-up of an object. When the monster and the man in the dumpster are tugging at the handgun and all we see is the gun and two hands. It is also an insert each time the shot only shows the tires skidding on the ground.

- **Continuity** – This is when the montage of shots shows progressive movement, action or generally makes us feel like things are going in order.

- **Straight Cut**- Every cut in this scene is a straight cut. There are no fancy transitions between any of the cuts. It is simply one shot connected to another shot.

- **Transition**- These are when a fade is used or some other transition between connected shots. Common transitions are fades, dissolves, wipes, and a myriad of other ones.

The challenge for this topic is that editing is much more intricate than these terms indicate. What I mean is that we also need to consider things like the pacing of the cuts. Most of the cuts in this scene come quickly. The editor obviously believed that it helps with the action and intensity of the scene. It feels faster paced. It might feel awkward if a laid-back conversation in a café were shot with quick cutting. The funny thing is that editors love to mess with the rules and will often work against some of these same terms to create a unique tone. Most editing and cuts feel so natural that we don't even know it is happening or don't notice it, until we do. It is at those points we should be paying attention even more closely and asking, "What did that mean?"

In splicing various shots of film together in a particular sequence an editor is not just telling a story. He or she is telling the director's story, conveying the director's message. An editor must also involve the audience by engaging them emotionally, intellectually, and oftentimes, spiritually. Editors do this by cutting on action, creating an eye-line match, using music and matching that with the visual. An editor controls the pace of the film, speeding it up with quicker, shorter clips, or slowing it down by adding longer shots. This assembling of shots takes one distinct shot and, in essence, creates a new meaning and/or a new understanding for the audience in the way it connects to the next original shot.

Think of a metaphor. The Bible is filled with them. God is described in metaphor; the church is described in metaphor. God is the good shepherd; the church is the bride of Christ. What do these metaphors do? They give us meaning. They place one entity (God) next to another dissimilar idea (good shepherd) and say they are alike, that they are connected. It tells us something of God's character.

Edits do a similar thing. They place one shot of film next to another shot and expect us to make connections, creating meaning, creating truth. And just as it is practically impossible to separate an understanding of God and His true character from the metaphors found in Scripture, it is difficult to separate the true message and meaning of a scene or a whole movie from the work an editor does. It is even more difficult to know how a different metaphor would affect our understanding. What if God had chosen different metaphors to describe himself? We would have a new or different understanding of who He truly is, just as a movie would have a different meaning with different edits.

So how do those connected shots in that order change or impact, help or hinder a director's original intention? It is difficult to say in a short series of bullet points. Editing is a complex process to explain because its impact is so vast. This is part of the difficulty in talking about editing. When we watch a film, it has already been assembled. We are seeing a finished product. We will only know the way that it exists now. This is important to remember because it also means we are seeing exactly what the filmmakers decided was the best way to convey their intentions, through emotions, ideas, concepts, action, and more.

There are occasional times where a director may re-edit a film and allow us an insight into "what may have been." Sometimes we can experience this through a Director's Cut version of a film. But even then, the mass of the film is not disrupted much and it has the same central idea and outcome as before. Every so often though a film comes along that gets a completely new meaning in a re-edit. Some films that come to mind are: ***Superman II: The Richard Donner Cut*** (2006), ***Blade Runner: 1992 Director's Cut*** (Ridley Scott-approved), and ***Donnie Darko: The Director's Cut*** (2004).

An editor can make or break a film in many cases. There are some that say editing is often more important than acting. I think there is a lot of truth to that statement. Alfred Hitchcock explains in this next clip the importance of editing and how it affects us as viewers. Let's see what he has to say.

Alfred Hitchcock on Editing

https://tinyurl.com/yau5a5sn

How do we handle this information? Did you see how the placement of one thing next to another changed its meaning? Were you thinking the same thing about the second montage, that he is a dirty old man? Of course you did. We all did. But what does that mean? Why are our minds so easily manipulated and convinced?

The effect he is talking about actually has a name and is called the **Kuleshov Effect**. It involves a series of simple shots that can have multiple meanings based on their arrangement. Our minds love to make assumptions and fill in gaps. We have been trained by years of watching screens. Henry David Thoreau talks about our minds in this way,

> "The surface of the earth is soft and impressible by the feet of men; and so with the paths which the mind travels. How ... deep the ruts of tradition and conformity!" (Thoreau, 2013)

The mind's paths are deep with ruts? This metaphor is saying that our minds are accustomed to patterns. Creatives, like movie directors, know this and they use it to their advantage. Directors know that we assume certain things. They know that we are familiar with certain types of shots, focus techniques, lighting, sound, camera angles and editing practices. So, moviemakers like to play around a little and mess with our minds, creating suspense, hooking us in, making us believe, creating empathy or repulsion. And we love it.

The question is, how does one explain editing in a practical way? I suppose the best way to explain it is to show what it is. Let me introduce you to one of the most discussed scenes when folks bring up film editing.

It is called the "Odessa Steps Sequence" from the 1925 Russian silent film **Battleship Potemkin**. This film and this scene are also known for its overt political message and is a perfect example of the way an editor must tell a story and convey a message all at once. If you have not seen it, this particular clip shows unarmed civilians standing along the high steps, joyfully watching and waving to the sailors in port just as an army of Cossacks in line behind them descend those steps with rifles firing indiscriminately.

Pay attention to how we get a sense of what is happening. Notice how the scene starts to establish setting and characters right away.

- How are the edits or cuts arranged?
- Are they quick cuts?
- Does the pace of the clip change?

Battleship Potemkin
The Odessa Steps

https://tinyurl.com/y8xl5wnm

The opening shot shows a busy harbor with boats, men, women, and sailors, loading food and supplies. Everyone is working together, and they are happy. The shot then changes to show steps filled with civilians - women and children, old people and cripples and they are happy, too. The people on the steps are looking in one direction - what are they looking at? We get our answer in the cutaway: The ships, the flags, the sailors. The shot cuts back again to the people. They seem like a good people.

Suddenly, soldiers arrive from above. We see them from a bird's-eye-view looking down on their line moving together. People start to flee. There is the side shot of people running. Which way are they running? On screen, it is from left to right. In these side shots, the lower part of the stairs is always on our right and the upper is always on our left. This is called **the 180-degree-rule**.

There is the tracking shot as the camera follows the people down the stairs (to the right). When people look up, they look to the left side of the screen. When they look downward they look to the right side of the screen. The edits back and forth show the emotion in their faces, the violence and running. This "Odessa Steps" clip is a scene that sits as an iconic section of cinema. This scene has been analyzed, adored and imitated for its power visually and its force metaphorically. It is propaganda in top form.

Editing the points of view can be a shot of an actor's face and/or a shot from their character's perspective. It can be done with a cutaway. Let me show you what I mean.

Apollo 13
Looking down

https://tinyurl.com/ybh7zkpd

By placing those shots together, we get the sense that Tom Hanks' character, even though he is in outer space, is looking right down into his own house on earth at his wife and that she is looking right up at him. We don't need words, just the connected shots of their points of view. Notice the 180-degree rule. He is shown looking down to the right and she is shown looking up to the left.

In this next scene, we go back to Hitchcock and watch the opening sequence of ***Rear Window***. There are a lot of extended shots and some quick cuts but see if you can't tell a little something about all the people that look down on that courtyard. How is Hitchcock setting the scene?

- What time of year is it?

Rear Window
Opening sequence

https://tinyurl.com/y7gmuqax

- Who is our main character?
- What does our main character do?

   Time and place are also important to the editing of a film. This next one is again from ***Citizen Kane.***

- How do we know this is in the past?
- What gives us the impression of time passing?

Citizen Kane
A marriage just like any other

https://tinyurl.com/y6wkgx6v

- Is it in real time or is the time compressed?
- Would you say it is slow-paced or fast paced?
- What is the director telling us about these two people in this montage?
- Did you notice all the changes?
- The size of the table, where they are sitting, their conversation? What is the message?

Next is a scene that is fairly fast-paced, introducing us to two little boys. What makes it fast-paced?

- What do you know about them by the end of the clip?
- Are they in America? If not, where are they?
- Does the music affect how we understand the clip?

Slumdog Millionaire
Boys on a Train

https://tinyurl.com/y8z3eszm

The clip that follows is also a fast-paced editing sequence from *Skyfall* that starts in on a motorcycle chase. Notice how most shots are barely more than one second long.

We begin with a motorcycle chase, then it is on the

Skyfall
Opening sequence,
motorbike chase

https://tinyurl.com/y8m42jh7

rooftops. Actually, it's two chases when you add the SUV on the street, and then there is a sudden shift in a crosscut from the chase to an office with people not at the chase. There are two distinct places. We have the quick cuts of the chase then suddenly, we are in an office with unrelated people in suits on a communication system and computers? These scenes are supposed to be happening simultaneously. How does this add to the tension of the chase?

The next clip in our editing section is even more manipulative. It does it all: The quick cut, cutting between time and place, using speculative ideas, using "real" historical film and facts. It goes from black and white to color and it uses repetition. It is violent. It utilizes sound and dialogue to make a point. It uses camera angles and movement, transitional blurs, focus and all sorts of other techniques. It is trying to tell us something. It is trying to convince us with an onslaught of visual rhetoric. The entire

The Good, the Bad and the Ugly
Three-way standoff

https://tinyurl.com/yd6st4fg

https://tinyurl.com/yahxrj33

movie is an argument by Oliver Stone about a conspiracy in the assassination of a president, John F, Kennedy, inspired by a real court trial in American history.

Editors will say that if you notice the editing as you watch a film then it is probably bad. The best editing is invisible, seamless. Except, of course, when it's not, like at the end of **The Good, the Bad and the Ugly**. This movie and this scene is the quintessential western stalemate ending. Except it isn't two men facing off on main street of town, it is one against one against one.

Three gunslingers vying for a chance at buried gold. Who is going to shoot whom? When? The constant cutting and the extreme close-ups of a face and an eye, a hand and gun. And, of course, the music.

Editing inescapably shapes a film's totality. The montage of shots creates its flow and course. It encompasses the arrangement of visuals into a whole. It contains the storytelling and the meaning. The editing process is about engagement of the viewer and the manipulation of the viewer. We yearn for great editing in sight and sound to create a feeling we won't soon forget.

RECAP

- Editing is the assembly of various shots into a particular order.

- Even though there are various techniques and terms and some rules, most editing is done by feeling, not formula.

- The better an editor knows the director's vision the better he or she can assemble the film.

- We see the movie as it is, not as it could have been.

- *In my YouTube channel for this chapter I have included a link to a short film entitled, "How Star Wars was saved in the edit," (https://tinyurl.com/y97ws8mt). It shows how a poorly edited early copy of the first **Star Wars** (1977) film could have easily ended up as forgettable junk but that a good team of editors were able to create a multibillion dollar franchise that will last decades. You can also get to it by using the QR code at the end of the chapter.*

- It could be argued that all films are saved in the edit.

- We are all subject to the Kuleshov Effect. Our brains

Unfortunately, internet links break. If any video link above does not work, check the link to my most updated YouTube playlist here:

EDITING

https://tinyurl.com/chapter-editing

are trained.

- Great editing can push us forward into the plot, create excitement, empathy, fear, happiness and all sorts of other emotions or it can allow us a reprieve from the tension. Even in old silent, foreign films we can see some of these techniques.

- The placing of shots next to one another is what brings meaning to a scene, a character, and essentially the movie as a whole.

- And a funny thing is, we oftentimes don't even need words to figure it out.

[11]

THE CONSPIRACY

I AM SURE YOU HAVE SEEN the seemingly endless names listed in any film's credits of individuals that made the movie you have just watched. To aid the director, these people plot and plan and scheme. They are the conspirators. They all worked together to manipulate your mind into believing something was funny, scary, interesting, sad, or suspenseful enough to make you laugh, cry, jump in your seat or sweat under your arms. This is their whole job. That is, if they did their job well.

In the midst of this the director worked to hold your attention so that you might better understand her vision of the world. How she sees things or how she thinks things work. The word "things" here refers to ideas like ethics, morals, relationships, winners, losers, authority, religion, science, politics, or whatever she wants. Through the action on the screen and the dialogue of the characters, the camera angles and lighting, the tone of the editing and the use of sound, the director constantly draws attention to these "things."

What sort of story does ***500 Days of Summer*** look like it

(500) Days of Summer
This is a story

https://tinyurl.com/y8w26e5c

will be? A teenager coming of age? A twenty-something trying to figure out life? A murder mystery? Will it be a character study or a high suspense action tale?

Remember what I said earlier, "It is not as much what the story does in the character, but what the story does in the viewer." All films start with story. Sometimes the story is original, and sometimes it comes from a source like a novel, a video game or another movie. Many stories will follow a sequence of events like the Hero's Journey (see Chapter 13). Either way, to make a film there was a story that at least one person believed needed to be told visually. A story that he believes will have meaning and purpose. A story that gives insight to the human condition or the way things should be. A plot that will inspire or create fear or make us understand ourselves a little better. Story is the starting point.

Documentaries, even those about penguins, use story to tell their information to the audience. Pay attention to the editing and music used in the trailer as well.

Because filmmakers are sometimes contrary folks they like to play with the typical constructs of story and filmmaking in order to bring their vision and meaning to light. In this next clip pay attention to who is telling the story. What happens with the characters? How does it

March of the Penguins
Trailer

https://tinyurl.com/y7lzwr28

affect the viewer? What sort of story will it be?

Stranger than Fiction
Harold Crick

https://tinyurl.com/yck9htdb

Story is powerful. Every story exists for a reason. What is the story? It is what God used to explain our whole history and what Jesus used to explain concepts like heaven, the kingdom of God, and grace. In film, a story becomes a script, a movie set, costumes and characters.

Every story needs a story teller. Who will tell the story of a film? The director. He will do it with the help of fellow conspirators like the editor, cinematographer, the set designer and the script. How does he see the world of the story and the characters that live in it? What is important to him, what needs to be left out, and any other idiosyncrasies along the way?

Princess Bride
A book

https://tinyurl.com/ybj52tlo

- How important is the storyteller in that last clip?
- Would the story still be told without the grandfather character?
- Would the meaning be the same?
- How do we get drawn into a story?
- What are filmmakers doing to bring us into their world?

Many filmmakers want to tell the audience about something challenging. This can be a daunting task.

Taking Chance
Trailer

https://tinyurl.com/y88lo7hu

- How does one tell about something particularly difficult?
- Or communicate to a difficult audience?

  In short, the answer is story.

Another idea to consider is the way the story is going to be told visually, or the how. The filmmakers will use all the techniques we have talked about and more. In film, the shots captured by the camera will tell us the story. Those images burned into film or digital memory will tell it. The camera does this with the help of lighting and sound, editing and acting. The camera catches it all. Through its lens we experience all the sights of the story of a film.

Lastly, in Tarantino's ***Kill Bill***, David Carradine's character, Bill, is not a particularly nice guy. Yet he does have an interesting idea. He wants to explore a story's meaning.

Kill Bill Vol.2
Superman stands alone

https://tinyurl.com/ydaolcjc

What does it mean that Superman's character is different than other superheroes? How is that important? This story is connected to the story arc of the movies *Kill Bill I & II*. It indicates that the movie itself has meaning larger than the plot.

What is the story of a movie telling us? We need to understand that we are being led by the moviemakers to watch their story. To be moved by it. It is the conspiracy. It isn't necessarily evil or bad. They want you to understand them, empathize with them and ultimately believe them.

By learning the film techniques discussed in this book you can now begin to use your understanding of them as tools to see the theme of each thing you watch. What its true message is. When you do this, people may think you are talking about weird new concepts. They may think you are making stuff up. The best way to justify your reasons is with evidence from the film. The next chapter is about where to look for this evidence. Because it isn't always about simply telling a nice story. These conspirators have an agenda. They may think their agenda is good and important. It might be the most amazing life inspiring event we have ever seen on screen. Their story may be filled with truth or fallacies. The only way we will know for sure is to check it up against the authority of Scripture. I find it a great pleasure to engage with those around me about a movie we have all watched, and to discuss the story, its ideas and the world views presented in the movie.

RECAP

- To make a movie it takes more than just the writer or the director or even the actors. There is a slew of people that make each movie.
- They are all collaborating together, conspiring to make something that others will watch, listen to and care about.
- They are telling a story. Stories are powerful. Even non-fiction documentaries use it.
- Filmmakers like to use story and the techniques of film to their advantage to tell us how they see the world and what it means.
- Story makes difficult ideas easier to tell and hear and see.
- Stories have meaning, and thus movies have meaning, we need to be watching and listening for the messages coming out of our screens.

Unfortunately, internet links break. If any video link above does not work, check the link to my most updated YouTube playlist here:

THE CONSPIRACY

https://tinyurl.com/chapter-conspiracy

[12]

THE SHAKEDOWN

MY HOPE IS THAT YOU NOW have some tools in your film watching tool box. I expect that you are beginning to enjoy movies on a new level. Now what? So what?

I want you to start using these tools in an effective way. I want to teach you how to shakedown a movie. How to hear and see what the movie is trying to communicate to you and what it wants you to believe. I liken it to interrogating it. Just know that the answers are not always clear or easy to get. Movies, as with books, do not readily tell you what they are about. That would be too easy and, frankly, too dreary. There are no special elves or fairies that come out at the end and tell you the moral of the story.

How do you "shakedown" the movie?

If we see the film as a structure built by the techniques of filmmaking how would we inspect it? How would we walk through its rooms and check it out? Now I am not talking about tying the movie to a chair and beating it with a hose like Billy Collins' bad English professor in his poem, "Introduction to Poetry". I just want us to be able to understand the message of the film as told by the director so that you can be clear about what you're being told. And so that you can run it up against Scripture.

Where do you start? What I have always appreciated is what I call *hand-holds*. I mean I can have all the equipment to climb a mountain, but if I don't have any beginning points or hand-holds I do not know how to get started. I have given you some equipment and now I am going to give you some hand-holds, some places to start using the tools to look for a film's meaning.

Here is a starting list of ideas to help you find meaning and help with creating discussion about a film:

1.You had me at the title or the opening credits.

Sometimes titles have hints as to the meaning in a movie. Sometimes they are merely descriptive like ***Top Gun*** (1986) or ***Casablanca*** (1942). Titles like ***To Kill a Mockingbird*** (1962), ***There Will Be Blood*** (2007), and I***nception*** (2010) definitely hint at some further meaning. Opening sequences to a movie can also give us hints as to a movie's meaning. There may be hints as to what is to come or secrets to a character's past or a mood we are supposed to be feeling. Consider films like any James Bond movie, ***Toy Story*** (1995), or ***Up*** (2009).

2. Where are we and when are we?

The setting, or where and when a story takes place, will influence the message of the film. What was happening historically at the time the activity of the film happens? Are we in a particular state or country? Maybe we are on a particular planet or an imaginary land. Are we in a prison, on an island, in an airplane? Why? Is it significant somehow? Just on this one level, the setting will affect the sorts of technology and knowledge characters have and the way they must solve problems. Consider these Tom Hanks films: *Cast Away* (2000), *Sully* (2016), *The Terminal* (2004), and *Captain Philips* (2013).

3. Where is everyone going (or, questioning the quest)?

The quest is important to storytelling. Is the main character(s) going somewhere? Are they looking for something or must they deliver something? Perhaps they must learn something along the way. Any film is a journey of discovery and growth for all involved, even us. Check out movies like: *Lord of the Rings*(2001-2003), *The Goonies* (1985), or *The Wizard of Oz* (1939).

Sometimes they are not going out, but rather they are trying to get home. Think: *Oh Brother Where Art Thou?* (2000), *Lion* (2016), or *The Incredible Journey* (1963).

Lion
Trailer

https://tinyurl.com/y8pjltnz

4.Wait a minute, I think I've seen something like this before.

Do you see something or sense something familiar? Better go check with Shakespeare, the Greeks and Romans, history, or the Bible (and if that doesn't work, go ask Disney).

Filmmakers love to use allusion and these are some of the places they get it from. Look at the number of characters, their names, names of places. You are looking for similar story patterns, things that may ring a bell. This could be parallel to or inspired by another movie or a book. Look for similar structures (not exact). Like *The Lion King* (1994) being the story of *Hamlet* (1990, 1996). Check out movies like: *Percy Jackson* (2010, 2013), *West Side Story* (1961), or *10 Things I Hate about You* (1999).

Sometimes the similarity is complex and hidden. Revisit the *Hellboy II* (2008) clip I showed you early on where the structure of those two characters looked out and one promised the world. Is it a parallel to Christ being tempted by Satan? Check out movies like: *The Matrix* (1999), *Iron*

Giant (1999), *E.T.* (1982), *Cool Hand Luke* (1967), or *One Flew Over the Cuckoo's Nest* (1975). I will discuss the Messiah structure in the next chapter.

a.   A plot by any other name.

Many times, a movie has been remade repeatedly. Check out movies like: *The Seven Samurai* (1954), *The Magnificent Seven* (1960), *A Bug's Life* (1998), *The Three Amigos* (1986), and *Galaxy Quest* (1999). These are all the same basic plot. Why does this plot have such appeal?

There are also movie pairs that share similar plots or copy plots exactly, like *Star Wars IV* (1977) and *The*

Seven Samurai
Trailer

https://tinyurl.com/y9yqjtk7

A Bug's Life
Trailer

https://tinyurl.com/ybve8q9c

Hidden Fortress (1958), *Yojimbo* (1961) and *Fist Full of Dollars* (1964), or *Rashomon* (1950) and *Hoodwinked!* (2005).

5. If it repeats, maybe it's a motif.

Things that are repeated inside a film itself could indicate a motif. Motif is in the repetition. Look for common colors, clothes, action, or objects or other structures within the film. The background often hides repetition in patterns, paintings, and pineapples. Repeated phrases or dialogue that says the same words or phrases over and over. Even the soundtrack could be a motif. Identifying motifs always lends to an understanding of the theme. Check out movies like: *The Sixth Sense* (1999), or *Inception* (2010).

6. Is he a good man or just a nice guy?

It is important that we as audience members understand the difference between a nice guy and an honorable man. A man that is honorable will have a moral code. He will stand for something. This code will most likely get tested and he'll be forced to assess, bend or break it. And he may not always be nice. A nice guy doesn't really stand for much. He pleases people and is a nice guy because he fears rejection, or he has little self-confidence. An honorable man may have some issues - he doesn't need to be perfect - but today's films like to blur the line of good and bad.

The Dark Knight
That's the rule you'll have to break

https://tinyurl.com/ybp3557n

a. Good, bad, I'm the guy with the cool name.

Sometimes there is something in that name. A deeper meaning. For instance, in **The Matrix** there are lots of interesting names: *Neo, Trinity*, and *Morpheus*. Character names with deeper meanings in other films may include **Solomon Kane (**2012), *Luke Skywalker, Darth Vader **(Star Wars** (1977)), - Katniss Everdeen (**The Hunger Games** (2012)), - John Coffey (JC) (**The Green Mile** (1999)), Anton Chigurh (not sweet = bitter or harsh) **(No Country for Old Men** (2007)),-,)- Jimmy Markum, Sean Devine (**Mystic River** (2003)).

b. There's nothing wrong with me, I was written that way for a reason.

Does someone have a unique birthmark or scar? Is there a sickness of the heart or the head? Is there an important character that is physically blind? Is the main character addicted to something? Is someone missing something like a hand or leg? Is someone expressly ugly or beautiful or small or large?

Check out movies like: ***Shrek*** (2001), ***Mask*** (1985), ***Hunchback of Notre Dame*** (various versions), ***Sherlock Holmes*** (2009), ***The Village*** (2004), ***The Sixth Sense*** (1999), or the ***Harry Potter*** series.

Mask
Rocky, what do you look like?

https://tinyurl.com/ycxcc722

The Village
I made a decision of the heart

https://tinyurl.com/yapov3e4

7. Does our hero have a weakness or a fear?

In literary terms, it is called an Achilles Heel or fatal flaw. Check out movies like: *Raiders of the Lost Ark* (1981), any *Superman* film, or *Unbreakable* (2000).

Raiders of the Lost Ark
Show a little backbone

https://tinyurl.com/y7jzvhpq

8. Who's eating together?

There are many studies out there about the significance of a shared meal, or a communion. Whether it is a family meal or a drink between strangers, food eaten together is important. Just as various ingredients are thrown together to make a tasty dish, a shared meal is its own recipe. Various flavors of characters thrown together to make a revealing scene. It is imperative to consider why a director would give movie time for characters to share a bite to eat. And even more striking is when the hero and the enemy sit together for a communion.

Check out movies like: *The Breakfast Club* (1985), *When Harry Met Sally* (1989), *Inglorious Basterds* (2009), *Alien* (1979), or *Hook* (1991). In many James Bond films, Bond often partakes of food and/or a beverage with the bad guy before their last conflict. In fact, *Babette's Feast* (1987) is all about a meal.

The Breakfast Club
Lunch

https://tinyurl.com/yalnp4m6

Babette's Feast
Trailer

https://tinyurl.com/y8s637vs

Dinners are so iconic and ubiquitous in film I couldn't help but throw a few more in for you:

More Dinners

https://tinyurl.com/yb5mtgvt

9. Did someone just give a speech?

What can I tell you, sometimes a character gives a speech. How important were the things that were said? Was there a clue to the movie's meaning and purpose?

Check out movies like: **Wall Street** (1987) when Gordon Gecko discourses on greed, or **Rocky Balboa** (2006) when Rocky talks to his son.

Wall Street
Greed is good

https://tinyurl.com/yb3nfasl

Rocky Balboa
Rocky talks to his son

https://tinyurl.com/rockyspeechson

10. Rain, snow and other bodies of water.

Water can be significant. It washes, it baptizes, and it weeps (well, sort of). Water is also a symbol of life. In the ***Harry Potter*** series, the "first years" get off the train and take a boat to Hogwarts. This is the only time they do this. Some would say that they are being marked by baptism into the Wizarding World.

Harry Potter and
The Sorcerer's Stone
Arrival

https://tinyurl.com/yc46fopp

11. Clanging Symbols, or "Gosh, that rings a bell" which means it might mean something.

Symbols are everywhere, I suppose, but be careful, if everything is symbolic then nothing is. Symbols often refer to general ideas or principles. A ring may signify a type of power but it may encircle your soul and keep you captive. See: ***Lord of the Rings*** (series), ***Inception***, **Superman** (various).

    a. Maybe you were just allegorizing?

Allegory is a little different than symbolism. Unlike symbols an allegory usually has a one to one meaning. In other words, that is the same as that. Check out movies like: ***The Chronicles of Narnia*** (Aslan=Christ, White Witch=Satan), ***Animal Farm*** (1954, 1999), ***Watership Down*** (1978), or ***The Life of Pi*** (2012).

12. Satan and the search for power

Occasionally Satan, a demon, or other underworldly entity appears as a character. He doesn't always have horns and hooves and "he" shows up as a "she" too. Usually this is a bad character but this isn't always true. If it is a bad guy it isn't always apparent at first because sometimes we think he is just the nice guy. Many times, he is good-looking, smart and wants to change things. He typically has what seem like fairly logical reasons for the change. He likes power or displays power. For example, politics are a place the Satan character likes to hang out. We also see the Satan character as a meddler, purveyor of fate, or some sort of person that messes with people's plans.

There is also the Satan-type character that is trying to make-good because directors and writers like to mess with assumptions. Check out movies like: **Hellboy** (2004, 2008) and **Spawn** (1997), or movies like: **The Passion of the Christ** (2004), **No Country for Old Men** (2007), **Devil** (2010), **Needful Things** (1993), **Something Wicked This Way Comes** (1983), **The Witches of Eastwick** (1987), **The Omen** (1976), or **The Devil's Advocate** (1997).

13. Did anyone learn anything new?

Something Wicked This Way Comes
Trailer (*Mr. Dark*)

https://tinyurl.com/ycaeh8we
https://tinyurl.com/ydhvmpwv

No Country for Old Men
Anton Chigurh

https://tinyurl.com/y9nbambp

Perhaps one of the characters had some sort of revelation? Did he or she come to a change of heart and mind? If so, what was their conclusion? Was it about truth or love? Did they become more cynical and bitter or was their heart broken and love spilled out? Remember, if a character explicitly learns something then we were supposed to learn that same thing... Or at least understand that what was learned was important and essentially good or right according to the movie makers. Check out movies like: ***Ocean's 11*** (1960, 2001), ***Shawshank Redemption*** (1994), ***The Green Mile*** (1999), or ***Stand by Me*** (1986).

14. Winners, losers and the rest of us.

Shawshank Redemption
Rehabilitated

https://tinyurl.com/yclal2ev

a.   Consequences...bad boys, bad boys, did they come for you? *Or did they let it slide?*

And what makes the bad guy so bad? I mean really?

Sometimes a bad guy will have a couple of attractive qualities but just because a bad guy seems appealing does not automatically make him okay. If a bank robber gets away with being a thief and there are no repercussions, does that make it okay to rob banks if you have really, really good reasons? We need to think about why a director/writer might do this. Check out movies like: ***Ocean's 11*** (2001), and ***Now You See Me*** (2013).

b. In the end, who lives, who dies, and who gets to eat the shawarma?

It may seem obvious but who lives and is free at the end is significant to the meaning of a film. If the good guys give up their cape or the bad guy walks away unnoticed this is important and purposeful.

The Avengers
End (edited)

https://tinyurl.com/yc37jguo

RECAP

- Here's a recap of just the 14 thematic points:

1. You had me at the title or the opening credits.
2. Where are we and when are we?
3. Where is everyone going (or questioning the quest)?
4. Wait a minute, I think I've seen something like this before.
   a. A plot by any other name.
5. If it repeats, maybe it's a motif.
6. Is he a good man or just a nice guy?
   a. Good, bad, I'm the guy with the cool name.
   b. There's nothing wrong with me, I was written that way for a reason.
7. Does our hero have a weakness or a fear?
8. Who's eating together?
9. Did someone just give a speech?
10. Rain, snow and other bodies of water.
11. Clanging Symbols, or "Gosh, that rings a bell" which means it might mean something.
    a. Maybe you were just allegorizing?
12. Satan and the search for power.
13. Did anyone learn anything new?
14. Winners, losers and the rest of us.
    a. Consequences...bad boys, bad boys, did they come for you? Or did they let it slide?
    b. In the end, who lives, who dies, and who gets to eat the shawarma?

Unfortunately, internet links break. If any video link above does not work, check the link to my most updated YouTube playlist is here:

SHAKEDOWN

https://tinyurl.com/chapter-shakedown

[13]

THE MONOMYTH

I REMEMBER A PROFESSOR in college that seriously challenged me. The class was called Christianity. I was at a secular university and sat in a room designed for about 40 people. On the first day, it was standing room only. I would bet there were over 100 people in there. This must have been a regular occurrence every semester because he gave what sounded like a prepared speech which was quite anti-Christian.

He said something like this, "If you are in this class because you think that somehow you are going to learn about how the Old and New Testament work together or how a man named Jesus supposedly died and was resurrected and is the fulfillment of mysterious prophesies then you are in the wrong classroom."

He continued to explain how this class was a study about the Myth of Christianity and not a place for those who think that they have some sort of faith or are, heaven forbid, "born again" to get any assurances or confidences about their beliefs. They would need to go to a church for that. He didn't pull any punches and he was quite rude in much of his first day dissertation. His weeding out process was quite effective. The next day there were about twenty students remaining.

I am not sure that this was the first time I heard Christianity referred to as a myth but this event sure sticks in my mind. I found it patronizing at best. I believe that the word "myth" is used by non-believers purposely to create an emotional arguing point in their favor and incite anger in those that have faith in Christ. If anyone were to challenge a professor like him on this point he would probably say in a condescending tone that myth refers to a story told about the history of a people that explains their origins, including things like religion, and that a myth can have truths.

When we talk about Greek and Roman Mythology everyone knows that these stories are not true, even though there may be truths in these stories about human nature and their relationships. The difference is that there never was a Zeus or Hercules or Medusa. There was, however, a Jesus of Nazareth, a King David and an Apostle Paul.

An intriguing ploy of the expert humanist or the college professor is the idea of the Monomyth as explained by Joseph Campbell. The Monomyth is also commonly referred to as the Hero's Journey. This Monomyth (one story) is a universal yet complete description of the journey all heroes take. Every hero's journey is just a variant of every other hero's journey. It is a sort of common cyclical sequence.

The sequence goes something like this: The hero is found in his status quo living in his ordinary world when he gets a call to adventure, receives wisdom and assistance, and departs his world by crossing a threshold or point of no return. He is thrust into a new world where various trials will test him, until the biggie, facing his worst fear. At this point things fall apart, he may face death and perhaps even die, but he is reborn, gaining a treasure or power or knowledge when he must return to his normal world. The Hero is forever changed, all the old ways of living don't work anymore and a new status quo begins. It doesn't take much experience in watching movies or reading stories to know that this Monomyth, or Hero's Journey, works in many of the stories we know. It may even be applied to our own lives.

Here is a nifty little film that explains it (Hey! Just because this is a cartoon does not mean we do not watch it for all the things we have been discussing all along here in this guide).

The secular humanist (non-believer) will often use the idea of the Hero's Journey to insist that because it is so

What Makes a Hero?
by Matthew Winkler

https://tinyurl.com/ycxjvynp

prevalent in history and in cultures around the world that it proves the story of Jesus is a myth. They say this because Jesus' story, which God felt the need to tell us in four different books, follows that Hero's Journey sequence quite well. For them, Jesus is just one more story in the tradition of a hero and his journey. Isn't it sort of ironic that a secularist will say that a well-designed structure such as the Monomyth discredits the existence of God or invalidates the Bible? They do not understand that Christians believe that God is the Great Designer. He is the creator of all things, including the concept of the Hero's Journey.

Brian Godawa puts it this way,

> *Christians need not deny a Monomyth that is reinterpreted through different traditions. We need only understand it in its true nature from God's own revelation. After all, God is the ultimate Storyteller, and the Scriptures say that He has placed a common knowledge of Himself in all people through creation and conscience. (Godawa, 2002)*

What Godawa is referring to of course can be found in the Bible:

> *For the wrath of God is revealed from heaven against all ungodliness and unrighteousness of men who suppress the truth in unrighteousness, because that which is known about God is evident within them; for God made it evident to them. For since the creation of the world His invisible attributes, His eternal power and divine nature, have been clearly seen, being understood through what has been made, so that they are without excuse. Romans 1:18-20 (ESV, 2001)*

> *For when Gentiles who do not have the Law do instinctively the things of the Law, these, not having the Law, are a law to themselves, in that they show the work of the Law written in their hearts, their conscience bearing witness and their*

thoughts alternately accusing or else defending them. Romans 2: 14, 15 (ESV, 2001)

Through these verses we understand this: Who God is is evident within all people, and that since the creation of the world the character traits of God have been clearly seen even though people cannot see God physically. When non-believers who do not treasure the law of God do any of the things it demands (like understanding that murder is bad or that we shouldn't steal), they show that the law is written on their hearts and that their conscience bears witness (tells the truth) to their thoughts which both accuse and defend them.

RECAP

- The word *myth* is a loaded term and can cause confusion.
- Joseph Campbell coined the term Monomyth.
- A monomyth is the idea that there is a general story about a hero that seems to span many people groups through history.
- The monomyth is also meant to represent our own journey.
- Jesus story appears to follow the monomyth. Yet the reality is that the monomyth points to the story of Jesus, not the other way around.

[14]

MESSIAH MANIFESTED

I WANT TO CONSIDER the prevalence of movies that use the Bible as a source or inspiration. These are movies that directly borrow or even steal ideas from Scripture. It is often called a Bible-Myth or Christ-Myth because the film will include forms or types from a Christian-like narrative or it will copy from the Bible itself. Remember, a myth is formed by combining truth with creative ideas to produce something new like poems, songs, paintings, other stories, and even movies. It may be a retelling of a biblical narrative or just a memory from some Sunday School class. Many films use ideas from the Bible or Christianity to contribute to the director's message about the meaning of life. A director may do this to either strengthen a biblical viewpoint or he will use the images to undermine and challenge it or try to discredit it.

If you are still confused, I apologize. Let me jump into some movies that may be familiar. There are movies that seem to be obvious or supportive of a biblical viewpoint. They are sincerely made Christian films from moviemakers like Kirk Cameron which may include titles like *Fireproof* (2008), *Mercy Rule* (2014), *Courageous* (2011), or *Facing the Giants* (2006). I am not talking about these. My focus here is more the mainstream films that have wide release and appeal. Movies like *Ben-Hur* (1959), *The Chronicles of Narnia* (2005-), *The Lord of the Rings* (2001-), *The Passion of the Christ* (2004), and *The Ten Commandments* (1956). These movies have been celebrated not only for being good or even great films but also for promoting an agenda that apparently supports Christian or biblical values.

Let's take a look at *Ben-Hur*. This was originally a book by a man named Lew Wallace. The book's full title is *Ben-Hur: A Tale of the Christ*. Wallace wanted to tell a story about a man, Ben-Hur, that encounters Jesus during various stages in his life. Here are a few clips:

Ben Hur
Meeting Jesus

https://tinyurl.com/yawdrbzw

Ben Hur
Water for Jesus

https://tinyurl.com/y6v6lfma

Those clips are from the popular 1959 film version, which is a remake of the 1925 silent film. Both movies have pretty cool non-CGI (computer generated image) chariot races.

Another set of films that have had appeal to a Christian audience are the movies made from the ***Chronicles of Narnia*** book series by C.S. Lewis: ***The Lion, the Witch and the Wardrobe*** (2005), ***Prince Caspian*** (2008), and ***The Voyage of the Dawn Treader*** (2010).

Due to the fact that Lewis was a well-known Christian and his books have biblical themes in allegorical form, many were thrilled to see them come to the big screen. This is also the reason books and films based on J.R.R. Tolkien's book like those in ***The Lord of the Rings*** series have great appeal. This next scene comes from The Lion, the Witch and the Wardrobe (2005), near the end, after Aslan has willingly given his life over to be a substitute for a boy facing death. The White Witch and all her minions have tortured and killed Aslan.

The Lion, the Witch and the Wardrobe
Aslan

https://tinyurl.com/yarvk63e

There are also movies that fall into a category that is not trying to hide their biblically-inspired narrative but their agenda seems to have more to do with modern application or singular appropriation of the biblical lesson. Movies like **Bruce Almighty** (2003) and **Evan Almighty** (2007) fall into this realm. In **Evan Almighty**, we encounter Evan in his normal life in the modern world becoming like Noah. He is charged by a character, called God, to build an ark. He is made fun of by all the people around him and his family struggles, but he builds it. Even though there is no rain forecasted the ark serves its good purpose. The next scene may be a spoiler if you haven't seen the movie.

Evan Almighty
The Ark and Congress

https://tinyurl.com/ycgrfesv

There are even movies that intentionally work with the mythology surrounding Judeo-Christian beliefs. **Raiders of the Lost Ark** is about the *Ark of the Covenant* or the special container that supposedly holds the remains of the original *Ten Commandments*. The description for the ark can be found in the Old Testament in Exodus 37:1-9.

Raiders of the Lost Ark
Exhuming the Ark

https://tinyurl.com/y8l4e96h

Another film along those same lines is **Indiana Jones and the Last Crusade**. This film explores the mythologies that surround the "cup of Christ" or the cup from which Jesus drank from at the Last Supper.

Then there are the films that are the not so obvious.

These films use multiple elements from the Bible or from Judeo-Christian heritage to create their own mythology. They will often have a messiah or Christ figure. We should be cautious of movies like these only because we do not want to fall into a trap. Just because we recognize elements of Christianity does not mean their agenda is necessarily to promote those values. In films such as *E.T.* and **Iron Giant** we see a sentient being come to us from afar. This being is misunderstood by many and connects deeply with a few. He performs miracles. He then gives up his life as a sacrifice, followed by a resurrection.

E.T.
Ouch

https://tinyurl.com/yblgt4xu

E.T.
He's Alive!

https://tinyurl.com/ydfkwv2u

The Iron Giant
Sacrifice

https://tinyurl.com/y8ulp3uq

The Iron Giant
Resurrection

https://tinyurl.com/yazbm5sh

TAKING A STROLL THROUGH *THE MATRIX* (1999)

A movie like this is intentionally philosophical in nature. It incorporates belief systems and theoretical ideas like billboards on a freeway. This is intentional. Many folks have argued that this film has many Christian elements and tells a Christian story. Now it is true that there are forms and types displayed in the film that mirror things from Christianity but it is not a Christian film. The next series of clips are from *The Matrix* (1999) and in them I highlight some of the things people generally point out to use as talking points. I will be adding some commentary of my own (*spoiler alert*).

The opening shot of the film is a green and black computer screen with numbers scrolling. Listen to the conversation. The voices talk about killing him and whether or not he is *The One, The Chosen*.

A little later we meet Neo and learn Neo might be the "One" (fun with anagrams). A group of people show up at Neo's door and they say some interesting things...

The Matrix
Opening sequence

https://tinyurl.com/y8attgsn

The Matrix
Halleluiah

https://tinyurl.com/ydex9c4r

Neo does some incredible things throughout the film and there is much discussion on whether or not he is the Chosen One. There are some exciting action sequences and

The Matrix
Last battle with Mr. Smith

https://tinyurl.com/yd2gvuor

the plot is interesting. There is a small group (most with cool names) of disciple-like people and out of that tight-knit

The Matrix
Neo Ascends (first 1:33 only)

https://tinyurl.com/yaww75fa

group one of them is a betrayer. Because of this betrayer, many of the group are killed. Towards the end of the film, Neo is in a battle with the baddie Mr. Smith. He is killed and then comes back to life. He must be the One. In fact, at the very end of the flick he ascends into heaven...

These scenes are all interesting and seem to copy or imitate sections from the Christian story but there are problems in this film if one wants to call it Christian. Big problems.

One of the largest holes, as far as a Christian story is concerned, is that Neo does not know who he is. He must discover himself like Herman Hesse's Siddhartha. Siddhartha contains teachings from both Hindu and Buddhist philosophies.

Another problem with this film is that it is a hodge-podge of all sorts of interesting belief systems. This film has no Christian agenda and instead blends Biblical forms into a mash-up of some manufactured belief system, making it more like the "COEXIST" bumper sticker seen on many Priuses.

All that being said, movies like **The Matrix** are great for creating conversation. I think that a movie like this should give us some caution, but never fear.

FLYING ON BROOMSTICKS THROUGH THE HARRY POTTER SERIES

There are movies that have all sorts of controversy surrounding them because of their content, like the **Harry Potter** series of books. They have witches and wizards, magical creatures and other fantastical things. It was always interesting that **The Lord of the Rings** got a pass on this stuff but **Harry Potter** was often considered evil because of it. (This in and of itself creates many enjoyable points of conversation.) I personally think JK Rowling was having some fun of her own because she throws in a big challenge and adds some subtle and not so subtle

Christological elements to her story. I have already mentioned the boats back in Chapter 10. But Harry, too, must sacrifice his life for others in the last of the series of books and movies. Warning, *spoilers* ahead.

And if you have been paying attention, you may already have guessed, he gets to be resurrected too, in order to defeat that Satan-looking character, "He who must not be

Harry Potter and
the Deathly Hallows Part 2
Harry Potter is...!

https://tinyurl.com/yanex4sx

named", Voldemort.

I do not think that this film is about promoting a Christian worldview but I also do not think it is undermining it either. It is merely utilizing a successful storyline. Many movies do this, especially superhero movies, from the Tobey Maguire **Spiderman** series, to **The Avengers** and **Superman** movies about a human-like being that comes to earth to be its savior.

There are all sorts of movies that employ Christian forms and types in order to tell their story. We have to be diligent in identifying them and equipping ourselves to talk about them. More movies in this category include: **Shawshank Redemption** (1994), **Gran Torino** (2008),

Babette's Feast (1987), *Se7en* (1995), *The Green Mile* (1999), *One Flew Over the Cuckoo's Nest* (1975), *The Revenant* (2015), and *Cool Hand Luke* (1967).

RECAP

- Myths aren't automatically bad or even untrue.
- There are a lot of beautiful artistic works inspired by the Bible.
- Many movies within the Christian film industry attempt to support a biblical viewpoint in their characters, plot and themes.
- There are even some popular films that also seem to have a broad appeal to people of faith.
- Many moviemakers use historical and or biblical ideas to form their possible vision of the world, sometimes they might take broad liberties.
- These stories may have some thematic elements from the Bible.
  - A character that performs miracles, they may die symbolically or for real and even come back to life.
- Finally, there are movies that appear to use ideas from the Bible or Christian sources yet intend to be subversive to the Christian worldview but at the same time.
- All of these movies require us to be diligent in our biblical discernment.

Unfortunately, internet links break. If any video link above does not work, check the link to my most updated YouTube playlist here:

MESSIAH MANIFEST

https://tinyurl.com/messiah-manifest

[15]

DENOUMENT

THE MAIN REVERIE PLAYING over and over in the dream factory of Hollywood is the song of optimism. It is louder than the tune Walt Whitman hears in his poem about America Singing. This is the dream of fantastic places and people, of possibility and potential.

What are the real messages coming out of the films we watch today? Is it that the little guy can always make it with straight gumption and grit? Bad guys, if they look good and have their heart in the right place, will be forgiven or given a token tap on the back of the hand? (Of course, if there is a bad guy that is truly evil, and I mean bad bad, then he will probably die in some memorable way, and he must realize just how bad he is as he dies. But who is that bad truly?)

Rugged individualism in life whether you are a police officer or entrepreneur is one of the best qualities you can have in film. Even if one begins as a non-English speaking immigrant, a bum on the street, or a minority abused and beaten, essentially a person with nothing, the message is often that you can have it all in the end which, by the way, is only about an hour away.

We can sing and dance in the rain, we can beat multiple evil henchmen whether they are in a stairwell or invading from outer-space. We can solve the greatest murder mystery or the most complex set of mathematical problems in the world. We can travel to any place or any time in the world or universe to find romance, life's meaning or great treasure.

One thing we must remember as we watch film is that we are hearing and seeing the dreams of those that have succeeded. Especially if we watch mostly popular films and blockbusters. Essentially, we are seeing the imaginings of millionaires. Most of the actors we see, and the directors we hear about, go home to a reality that is at the far edge of most of our dreams. They are the philosophers of our time, throwing their ideas up on a screen and seeing if they will seep in. These stories are their stories and that is why we must understand them. The challenges that characters go through on-screen end when the cameras stop rolling. The bruises and bullet holes get wiped off. These people have their normal lives. But their normal life is often in the realm of our dreams. This is why there are so many TV shows dedicated to telling the masses about their extravagant lives.

Many of us see it so often that we are a little like the men chained in Plato's cave. Whether we want to acknowledge it or not several of us have begun to believe that these images projected on the dark wall of the cinema's cave are real. The funny part is that we willingly believe this even though we are not technically chained. But that screen has been there most of our lives.

Filmmakers make films based on the people that they are or how they perceive the world of the everyman. They see life in their way through their mind's eye. Just know that a film about a young school teacher in an inner-city school is not the true-life story of that school teacher, or any school teacher for that matter. It is a type or form of teacher. It looks real, sounds real and feels real, but in the end the apple gets tossed out and those students aren't using those text books or writing notes. They are props.

What does that tell us about film? About us? What does it mean?

These perhaps are the bigger issues around film and some of these things we don't want to think about. Maybe there are complaints about how much money is being paid or made but we buy the tickets and the subscriptions. We wear the clothes and purchase the products displayed in the background.

Let's not be deceived. The normal life of a millionaire is not always the American Dream either. They have bad breath and bad hair days, too. They have arguments with their spouse and deal with children and dirty diapers. They have divorce. Money, for all its promises, does not care for any of us. It does not love us or stay up late nights or work sixty hours a week for us.

What are the messages coming out of the screens we watch? They are powerful, meaningful and seem so right, and so possible. Your neighbor and co-worker are hearing those same messages. Are the messages good? Are they hopeful? What is that hope in?

In Hollywood conflict is king. The story needs to keep moving, so throw in a plot device: Argument, affair, sickness, car trouble, death, murder. There are no real movies about a normal family with normal kids and a normal life where parents go to work, do their job and come home to dinner. Where kids run off to school, come home, do homework and go to bed. This sort of life is normal but in movies it is non-existent. It's boring. Life is not boring but in movies, real life is.

In movies, there are affairs lurking in the dark corners of the office, and lunch room fights at school, or drama in the locker room. There is a horrible car crash or a kidnapping at the mall. These things are a rarity in reality but in the movies they are all the rage. Especially if it is based on, or inspired by, true events. Many people think that their life is doldrum and blasé. That if they don't have drama and conflict then it's a waste of time. These people believe that reality shows are real and that having money will solve all their problems. This is the sort of fare we watch along with our neighbors and coworkers and our kids. (Have you watched a Disney TV show lately? Even fifth graders need a boyfriend or girlfriend.)

As believers we must keep our center. Like Huckleberry Finn keeps returning to his father figure, Jim, on the raft in the river of his life, we must also return to the source of light, our Father of Life, found in the pages of the Bible. If we do not see clearly with the Bible as our filter, we will get caught up in the waves of conflict we are told our lives should be full of and forget Jesus' words about who is blessed: Peacemakers and the poor in spirit, the merciful and pure in heart. We are to be salt and light to this world. Like the light that shines out of the screen in a dark room we need to bridge the gap from light to the light of God. Sometimes I think we could find our lives much like Ray Bradbury's Leonard Mead in the short story "The Pedestrian" as he walks around his neighborhood, houses lit from the inside by televisions at night.

And on his way, he would see the cottages and homes with their dark windows, and it was not unequal to walking through a graveyard where only the faintest glimmers of firefly light appeared in flickers behind the windows. Sudden gray phantoms seemed to manifest upon inner room walls where a curtain was still undrawn against the night, or there were whisperings and murmurs where a window in a tomblike building was still open. (Bradbury, The Pedestrian, 1951)

We should not let our neighborhood become a graveyard or our office a mausoleum. We need to be salt and light to those around us.

To illustrate this, I have included the following beautiful short film from Belgian filmmaker Guy Thys. It is commonly known by the title ***Tanghi Argentini*** (***Argentine Tangos***).

Watching movies and television shows to have discussions with people is not the sole way to be salt and

Tanghi Argentini
A short film

https://tinyurl.com/TanghiArgentini

light. Get to know those we are around and offer them your friendship. We need only say hello. And maybe have a chat about a movie.

BIBLIOGRAPHY

Bradbury, R. (1951, August 7). The Pedestrian. (M. Ascoli, Ed.) *The Reporter*, pp. 39-42. Retrieved July 13, 2018, from http://www.unz.com/print/Reporter-1951aug07-00039/

Bradbury, R. (1995). *Fahrenheit 451.* New York: Simon & Schuster Paperbacks.

ESV. (2001). *The ESV Bible (The Holy Bible, English Standard Version).* Wheaton, Illinois: Crossway a publishing ministry of Good News Publishers.

Foster, T. C. (2003). *How to Read Literature Like a Professor.* New York: Harper Collins Publishers Inc.

Giannetti, L. (2008). *Understanding Movies* (11th ed.). Upper Saddle River: Pearson Prentice Hall.

Godawa, B. (2002). Hollywood Worldviews Watching Films with Discernment & Wisdom. Downers Grove, IL: InterVarsity Press.

Pramaggiore, M., & Wallis, T. (2008). *Film a Critical Introduction* (2nd ed.). City Road, London: Laurence King Publishing Ltd.

Prince, S. (2010). *Movies and Meaning an Introduction to Film* (5th ed.). Boston: Pearson Education, Inc. as Allyn and Bacon.

Ryken, L. (1986). *Culture in Christian Perspective.* Portland: Multnomah Press.

Schaeffer, F. (1982, February 2). The Battle for our Culture. pp. 4-9. (N. W. Magazine, Interviewer) Retrieved July 13, 2018, from http://www.samizdat.qc.ca/arts/FS_cult_e.htm

Schaeffer, F. (1990). *Sham Pearls for Real Swine .* Aurora: Wolgemuth & Hyatt Publishers Inc.

Thoreau, H. D. (2013). *Walden, and On The Duty Of Civil Disobedience.* Project Gutenberg. Retrieved July 13, 2018, from http://www.gutenberg.org/files/205/205-h/205-h.htm

INDEX OF FILM CLIPS